MW01268956

The Book of Baking Bread
Master the Art of Sourdough, Pastry, Yeast, and Easy Recipes

Ebony Irvyn

This Book Belongs to:

_____

_____

_____

Thanks ever so much to each of my cherished readers for investing the time to read this book!

I know you could have picked from many other books, but you chose this one. So, a big thanks for reading all the way to the end. If you enjoyed this book or received value from it, I'd like to ask you for a favor. Please take a few minutes to **post an honest and heartfelt review on** Amazon.com. Your support does make a difference and helps to benefit other people.

Thanks!

Table of Contents

SUMMARY 1

Copyright 6

INSTEAD OF PROLOGUE 27

What to do to make the cooking process understandable for everyone? 28

PROFESSOR RAYMOND CALVEL AND HIS METHOD 30

THE INFLUENCE OF INGREDIENTS ON BREAD 31

METHOD OF MAKING SOURDOUGH STARTER WITH WHEAT AND RYE FLOUR 33

METHOD OF AUTOLYSE OF PROFESSOR RAYMOND CALVEL 37

PROFESSOR RAYMOND CALVEL'S RYE AND WHEAT BREAD 40

WHAT WE WILL NEED TO START MAKING BREAD AND WHAT IS IMPORTANT TO KNOW ABOUT IT? 44

TECHNOLOGY OF MAKING BREAD 46

HEALTHY SOURDOUGH BREAD 47

HOW TO MAKE SIMPLE SOURDOUGH STARTER? 48

HOW TO REFRESH SOURDOUGH STARTER? 49

AUTOLYSE 50

CACAO SOURDOUGH BREAD WITH RAISINS 53

FRENCH VILLAGE SOURDOUGH BREAD 58

OAT & WHEAT SOURDOUGH BREAD 62

BUCKWHEAT GRAIN BREAD WITH PUMPKIN SEEDS 66

BRAN SOURDOUGH BREAD 70

PUMPKIN SOURDOUGH BREAD 74

RYE SOURDOUGH BREAD 78

WHEAT AND OAT SOURDOUGH BREAD WITH OLIVES 82

WHOLEGRAIN WHEAT BREAD WITH LINEN AND SUNFLOWER SEEDS 86

TRADITIONAL SOURDOUGH BAGUETTE 90

WHEAT & RYE BREAD WITH MIXED SEEDS 94

FOCACCIA WITH OLIVES AND SUN-DRIED TOMATOES 98
HOW TO MAKE DOUGH WITH YEAST 102
HEALTHY RYE & BRAN BREAD WITH ROSEMARY AND OLIVES 104
ONION BREAD 108
RYE BREAD ROLLS 112

SIMPLE SANDWICH BREAD	116
BASBOUSA	121
FOCACCIA BREAD WITH SUNDRIED TOMATOES AND OLIVES	126
CINNABONS	132
BREAKFAST SESAME BUNS	137
STRAWBERRY JAM	141
TRADITIONAL JEWISH BREAD CHALLAH	144
ORANGE GINGER CAKE	148
HOMEMADE BURGER BUNS	152
CINNAMON BUNS	156
VEGAN STEAMED BUNS WITH APPLE AND PEAR FILLING	160
FLUFFY BUNS WITH CARAMELIZED APPLES & CRUMBLE	165
BIRD BREAD	172
BAGELS	176
CINNAMON TWISTED BREAD	183
LIVE WITHOUT GLUTEN	187
WHY GLUTEN IS HARMFUL?	189
GLUTEN FREE DARK BREAD	190
GLUTEN FREE GREEN BUCKWHEAT BREAD	194
GLUTEN FREE ZUCCHINI BREAD	198
STIR - FRIED VEGETABLES WITH FRESH HERBS	202
GLUTEN FREE SANDWICH BREAD	206
STRAWBERRY CONFITURE	210
CHOCOLATE GLUTEN FREE MUFFINS WITH FROSTING	214
GLUTEN FREE SCONES WITH POPPY SEEDS	219
OAT BREAKFAST MUFFINS WITH DRIED APRICOTS	224
LEMON DRIZZLE CAKE	228
METRIC CONVERSION CHARTS	233

Summary

"The Timeless Art of Bread Baking: This is a comprehensive guide that delves into the intricate world of bread making. This book is a treasure trove of knowledge for both novice bakers and seasoned professionals, offering a wealth of information on the history, techniques, and science behind the art of bread baking.

The author takes readers on a journey through time, exploring the origins of bread and its significance in various cultures. From ancient civilizations to modern-day bakeries, the book provides a fascinating account of how bread has evolved over centuries, reflecting the diverse culinary traditions and innovations that have shaped this staple food.

One of the standout features of this book is its emphasis on technique. The author meticulously breaks down each step of the bread baking process, from selecting the right ingredients to mastering the art of kneading and shaping dough. With clear and concise instructions, accompanied by detailed illustrations, readers are guided through the intricacies of bread making, ensuring that they can replicate the recipes with precision and confidence.

Furthermore, ""The Timeless Art of Bread Baking"" goes beyond the basics, delving into the science behind bread making. The author explains the role of different ingredients, such as yeast and flour, and how they interact to create the perfect loaf. This scientific approach not only enhances readers' understanding of the bread making process but also empowers them to experiment and adapt recipes to suit their preferences.

In addition to the technical aspects, this book also celebrates the artistry and creativity involved in bread baking. The author showcases a wide range of bread recipes, from classic sourdough and baguettes to more exotic variations like focaccia and brioche. Each recipe is accompanied by stunning photographs that capture the beauty and allure of freshly baked bread, inspiring readers to embark on their own culinary adventures.

""The Timeless Art of Bread Baking"" is not just a cookbook; it is a comprehensive resource that equips readers with the knowledge and skills to become proficient bread bakers. Whether you are a passionate home cook or a professional baker, this book is a must-have addition to your culinary library. With its meticulous attention to detail, historical insights, and practical guidance, it is sure to become a cherished companion on your bread baking journey."

"The Spectrum of Bread: From Sourdough to Gluten-Free: The spectrum of bread is incredibly diverse, ranging from traditional sourdough loaves to modern gluten-free options. Bread has been a staple food for centuries, and its evolution has been shaped by cultural, dietary, and health considerations.

Sourdough bread, with its tangy flavor and chewy texture, is one of the oldest forms of bread. It is made through a natural fermentation process, where wild yeast and bacteria break down the carbohydrates in the dough, resulting in a unique flavor profile. Sourdough bread is often praised for its health benefits, as the fermentation process increases the bioavailability of nutrients and reduces the glycemic index, making it easier to digest and less likely to cause blood sugar spikes.

Moving along the spectrum, we encounter whole grain bread. This type of bread is made from flour that contains the entire grain, including the bran, germ, and endosperm. Whole grain bread is rich in fiber, vitamins, and minerals, making it a nutritious choice. It has a denser texture and a nuttier flavor compared to white bread, which is made from refined flour that has had the bran and germ removed.

As we progress further, we come across artisan bread. Artisan bread is typically handmade by skilled bakers using traditional methods and high-quality ingredients. It often incorporates specialty flours, such as rye or spelt, and may feature unique flavorings like herbs, nuts, or dried fruits. Artisan bread is known for its crusty exterior, soft interior, and complex flavors, making it a favorite among bread enthusiasts.

In recent years, the demand for gluten-free bread has skyrocketed due to the increasing prevalence of gluten intolerance and celiac disease. Gluten is a protein found in wheat, barley, and rye, and can cause digestive issues and inflammation in individuals with gluten-related disorders. Gluten-free bread is made using alternative flours, such as rice, corn, or almond flour, and often requires additional ingredients like xanthan gum or psyllium husk to mimic the texture and elasticity of gluten-containing bread.

Beyond these examples, the spectrum of bread continues to expand with various specialty breads, such as flatbreads, bagels, brioche, and more. Each type of bread offers its own unique characteristics, flavors, and textures, catering to different tastes and dietary needs.

In conclusion, the spectrum of bread is vast and diverse, ranging from traditional sourdough to modern gluten-free options. "

"Purpose and Structure of Bread Baking Book: The purpose of a bread baking book is to provide readers with a comprehensive guide on how to bake various types of bread, from basic loaves to more complex artisanal creations. The book aims to educate and inspire both novice and experienced bakers, offering step-by-step instructions, tips, and techniques to help them achieve successful results.

The structure of a bread baking book typically follows a logical progression, starting with an introduction that provides an overview of the bread baking process and the essential ingredients and equipment needed. This section may also include information on the history and cultural significance of bread, as well as the health benefits of homemade bread.

The book then moves on to the main body, which is usually divided into chapters based on different types of bread. Each chapter focuses on a specific category, such as white bread, whole wheat bread, sourdough bread, or specialty breads like baguettes or brioche. Within each chapter, the author provides detailed recipes for different variations of the bread type, along with variations in ingredients and techniques to cater to different tastes and dietary preferences.

In addition to the recipes, the book may also include sections on essential techniques and skills, such as kneading, shaping, proofing, and baking. These sections provide detailed instructions and illustrations to help readers master the fundamental techniques required for successful bread baking.

Furthermore, a bread baking book may also include troubleshooting guides, where the author addresses common issues that bakers may encounter during the bread baking process. This section offers solutions and tips to overcome challenges, such as dough that doesn't rise properly, bread that turns out too dense or dry, or crust that doesn't brown evenly.

To enhance the reader's understanding and enjoyment of the bread baking process, many books also include beautiful photographs or illustrations of the finished breads, as well as step-by-step visual guides for key techniques. These visuals not only serve as a source of inspiration but also help readers visualize the desired outcome and ensure they are on the right track.

Finally, a bread baking book may conclude with additional resources, such as a glossary of baking terms, a list of recommended baking tools and equipment, and suggestions for further reading or exploring advanced bread baking techniques.

Overall, the purpose and structure of a bread baking book are to provide readers with a comprehensive and accessible guide to baking delicious bread at home. By combining detailed recipes, essential techniques, troubleshooting guides, and visual aids, these books empower bakers of all levels to create their own homemade bread with confidence"

"How to Navigate This Comprehensive Bread Baking Guide: Welcome to our comprehensive bread baking guide! Whether you're a beginner or an experienced baker, this guide will provide you with all the information you need to successfully bake delicious bread at home.

To navigate through this guide, we have organized the information into several sections. Each section focuses on a specific aspect of bread baking, allowing you to easily find the information you're looking for.

First, we have the ""Ingredients"" section. Here, you will learn about the essential ingredients needed for bread baking, such as flour, yeast, salt, and water. We will discuss the different types of flour and their characteristics, as well as the role of yeast in bread fermentation.

Additionally, we will provide tips on selecting the best ingredients for optimal bread quality.

Next, we move on to the ""Equipment"" section. In this section, we will cover the various tools and equipment you'll need for bread baking. From mixing bowls and measuring cups to bread pans and ovens, we will guide you through the essential equipment required for successful bread making. We will also provide recommendations on high-quality equipment that can enhance your baking experience.

Once you have gathered your ingredients and equipment, it's time to dive into the ""Bread Making Techniques"" section. Here, we will walk you through the step-by-step process of making bread from scratch. We will cover topics such as mixing and kneading the dough, proofing and shaping the bread, and finally, baking it to perfection. Along the way, we will share valuable tips and tricks to help you achieve the best results.

In the ""Troubleshooting"" section, we address common issues that may arise during the bread baking process. From dense and flat loaves to overproofed or underproofed dough, we will provide solutions to help you troubleshoot and overcome these challenges. We understand that baking can sometimes be unpredictable, but with our troubleshooting tips, you'll be able to tackle any problem that comes your way.

Lastly, we have the ""Recipes"" section. Here, you will find a collection of tried and tested bread recipes that you can try at home. From classic white bread to artisan sourdough, we have a variety of recipes to suit different tastes and preferences. Each recipe includes detailed instructions and ingredient measurements, ensuring that you can recreate the bread successfully.

Throughout this comprehensive bread baking guide, we have included helpful illustrations and photographs to visually guide you through the process. We believe that visual aids can greatly enhance your understanding and make the"

"Understanding the Science of Bread Baking: Bread baking is not just a simple process of mixing ingredients and putting them in the oven. It is a complex science that involves understanding the chemical reactions and physical changes that occur during the baking process.

One of the key ingredients in bread baking is flour. Flour is made up of proteins, starches, and other components. When flour is mixed with water, the proteins in the flour form gluten. Gluten is a network of proteins that gives bread its structure and elasticity. It is what allows the dough to rise and hold its shape during baking.

Yeast is another important ingredient in bread baking. Yeast is a microorganism that feeds on the sugars in the dough and produces carbon dioxide gas as a byproduct. This gas gets trapped in the gluten network, causing the dough to rise. The yeast also produces alcohol and other flavor compounds that contribute to the taste and aroma of the bread.

The process of bread baking involves several stages. First, the ingredients are mixed together to form a dough. This dough is then kneaded to develop the gluten and distribute the yeast evenly. Kneading also helps to incorporate air into the dough, which aids in the rising process.

After kneading, the dough is left to rise, or ferment, for a period of time. During this time, the yeast continues to feed on the sugars in the dough and produce carbon dioxide gas. The gluten network traps the gas, causing the dough to expand and rise.

Once the dough has risen, it is shaped into the desired form, such as a loaf or rolls. It is then left to rise again, known as the proofing stage. This allows the dough to relax and further develop its flavor.

Finally, the dough is baked in an oven. The heat of the oven causes the carbon dioxide gas to expand even further, resulting in a light and airy texture. The heat also causes the proteins in the dough to denature and set, giving the bread its final structure.

Understanding the science of bread baking allows bakers to make adjustments and troubleshoot any issues that may arise. For example, if the bread is not rising properly, it may be due to a lack of gluten development or insufficient fermentation time. By understanding the underlying principles, bakers can make adjustments to the recipe or technique to achieve the desired result.

In conclusion, bread baking is a fascinating science that involves understanding the chemical reactions and physical changes that occur during the baking process. "

"Essential Ingredients and Equipment for Baking Bread: When it comes to baking bread, there are a few essential ingredients and equipment that you will need to ensure successful results. Let's dive into the details of each one.

First and foremost, the key ingredient for baking bread is flour. All-purpose flour is commonly used for most bread recipes, but you can also experiment with different types such as whole wheat, rye, or even gluten-free flour for dietary restrictions. The type of flour you choose will affect the texture and flavor of your bread, so it's important to select the right one for your desired outcome.

Another crucial ingredient is yeast. Yeast is responsible for the fermentation process that gives bread its airy and fluffy texture. There are two main types of yeast: active dry yeast and instant yeast. Active dry yeast needs to be dissolved in warm water before use, while instant yeast can be added directly to the dough. Both types work well, but it's important to follow the instructions on the package to ensure proper activation.

Salt is another essential ingredient in bread baking. It not only enhances the flavor but also helps to control the fermentation process. Salt slows down the activity of yeast, preventing the dough from rising too quickly and resulting in a more balanced flavor. Be sure to use the right amount of salt specified in the recipe to achieve the desired taste.

Water is the primary liquid used in bread dough. It helps to hydrate the flour and activate the yeast. The temperature of the water is crucial, as it affects the fermentation process. Most recipes call for warm water, around 105°F to 115°F, to activate the yeast. However, it's important to note that different types of yeast may require different water temperatures, so always refer to the specific instructions.

In addition to these essential ingredients, there are a few optional ingredients that can enhance the flavor and texture of your bread. Sugar or honey can be added to provide sweetness and help activate the yeast. Fats, such as butter or oil, can be used to add richness and moisture to the bread. Eggs can also be added to enrich the dough and create a softer texture.

Now let's move on to the equipment needed for baking bread. The most basic equipment you'll need is a mixing bowl and a wooden spoon or a stand mixer with a dough hook attachment. These tools are used to combine the ingredients and knead the dough. Kneading is an important step in bread baking as it develops the gluten, which gives the bread its structure and elasticity."

"The Role of Flour, Yeast, Water, and Salt in Bread Making: Bread making is a fascinating process that involves several key ingredients, including flour, yeast, water, and salt. Each of these ingredients plays a crucial role in creating the perfect loaf of bread, and understanding their individual functions is essential for achieving the desired outcome.

Flour is the main ingredient in bread making and provides the structure and texture of the final product. It is typically made from ground grains, such as wheat, rye, or barley. The proteins in flour, specifically gluten, are responsible for giving bread its elasticity and chewiness. When flour is mixed with water, gluten forms and creates a network of strands that trap carbon dioxide produced by yeast during fermentation. This process, known as gluten development, gives bread its characteristic airy and light texture.

Yeast is another vital ingredient in bread making. It is a microorganism that feeds on sugars and produces carbon dioxide and alcohol as byproducts. Yeast is responsible for the fermentation process, which is crucial for bread to rise. When yeast is mixed with warm water and a small amount of sugar, it becomes activated and starts to multiply. As the yeast consumes the sugar, it releases carbon dioxide gas, causing the dough to expand and rise. This process is essential for creating the airy and fluffy texture of bread.

Water is a fundamental component in bread making as it hydrates the flour and activates the yeast. The temperature of the water is crucial, as it affects the fermentation process. Warm water, around 100-110°F (38-43°C), is typically used to activate the yeast and promote its growth. Cold water can slow down the fermentation process, while hot water can kill the yeast. Additionally, water helps to dissolve the salt and distribute it evenly throughout the dough, enhancing the flavor of the bread.

Salt may seem like a small ingredient, but it plays a significant role in bread making. It not only enhances the flavor of the bread but also regulates the fermentation process. Salt helps to control the activity of yeast, preventing it from fermenting too quickly and producing an overly gassy dough. It also strengthens the gluten structure, allowing the dough to hold its shape during rising and baking. Furthermore, salt acts as a natural preservative, extending the shelf life of bread by inhibiting the growth of mold and bacteria.

In conclusion, the role of flour, yeast, water, and salt in bread making is crucial for creating the perfect loaf of bread. Flour provides the structure and texture, yeast ferments the dough and causes"

"Basic Techniques: Kneading, Proofing, and Baking of Bread Baking: Bread baking is an art that requires a combination of basic techniques to achieve the perfect loaf. Three essential techniques in bread baking are kneading, proofing, and baking.

Kneading is the process of working the dough to develop gluten, which gives bread its structure and elasticity. It involves repeatedly folding, pressing, and stretching the dough to activate the gluten strands. Kneading can be done by hand or with the help of a stand mixer. By kneading the dough, you are redistributing the yeast and allowing it to ferment evenly throughout the dough. This process also helps to incorporate air into the dough, resulting in a lighter and fluffier texture. Kneading is typically done until the dough becomes smooth, elastic, and springs back when pressed with a finger.

Proofing, also known as fermentation, is the crucial step where the dough rises and develops its flavor. During proofing, the yeast in the dough consumes the sugars and produces carbon dioxide gas, causing the dough to expand. This process takes place in a warm and humid environment, usually at room temperature or slightly higher. Proofing allows the dough to relax and develop its gluten structure further. It also enhances the flavor and aroma of the bread as the yeast produces various compounds during fermentation. The duration of proofing can vary depending on the recipe, but it typically takes around 1-2 hours.

Once the dough has been kneaded and proofed, it is ready for baking. Baking bread involves placing the dough in a preheated oven and subjecting it to high heat. The heat causes the carbon dioxide gas trapped in the dough to expand further, resulting in the bread's final rise. Baking also creates a golden crust on the outside of the bread, which adds texture and flavor. The temperature and baking time can vary depending on the type of bread being baked. Generally, bread is baked at a high temperature initially to create a burst of steam, which helps the bread rise and develop a crisp crust. The temperature is then reduced to allow the bread to bake evenly without burning.

In conclusion, bread baking requires a combination of basic techniques such as kneading, proofing, and baking. Kneading develops gluten and creates a smooth and elastic dough. Proofing allows the dough to rise, develop flavor, and relax its gluten structure. Baking gives the bread its final rise, creates a golden crust, and ensures even cooking. Mastering these techniques is essential for achieving delicious and perfectly baked"

"The Art and Science of Sourdough of Bread Baking: The Art and Science of Sourdough Bread Baking is a comprehensive guide that delves into the intricate world of sourdough bread making. This book is a must-have for both novice and experienced bakers who are looking to master the art of creating delicious and flavorful sourdough bread.

The author takes a scientific approach to sourdough bread baking, providing readers with a deep understanding of the fermentation process and the role it plays in creating the unique taste and texture of sourdough bread. The book explores the science behind the wild yeast and bacteria that naturally occur in sourdough starters, explaining how they interact to produce the characteristic tangy flavor and chewy texture that sourdough bread is known for.

In addition to the science, the author also delves into the artistry of sourdough bread baking. The book provides detailed instructions on how to create and maintain a sourdough starter, which is the foundation of any successful sourdough bread. The author shares their personal tips and tricks for achieving the perfect balance of acidity and flavor in the starter, as well as how to troubleshoot common issues that may arise during the fermentation process.

The Art and Science of Sourdough Bread Baking also covers a wide range of sourdough bread recipes, from classic country loaves to more adventurous variations like olive and rosemary sourdough. Each recipe is accompanied by step-by-step instructions and helpful tips, ensuring that even the most novice baker can successfully create a delicious loaf of sourdough bread.

What sets this book apart from others on the subject is the author's passion for sourdough bread baking. Their enthusiasm shines through in every page, making the book not only informative but also inspiring. The author's love for the craft is contagious, and readers will find themselves eager to dive into the world of sourdough bread baking.

Whether you are a seasoned baker looking to expand your repertoire or a beginner just starting out, The Art and Science of Sourdough Bread Baking is an invaluable resource. With its detailed explanations, practical tips, and mouthwatering recipes, this book is sure to become a staple in any baker's kitchen. So grab your apron and get ready to embark on a delicious journey into the world of sourdough bread baking."

"Creating and Maintaining a Sourdough Starter of Bread Baking: Creating and maintaining a sourdough starter is an essential step in the process of bread baking. A sourdough starter is a mixture of flour and water that is left to ferment, allowing wild yeast and bacteria to develop. This natural fermentation process gives sourdough bread its distinct flavor, texture, and rise.

To create a sourdough starter, you will need a few simple ingredients: flour, water, and time. Start by combining equal parts of flour and water in a clean container. It is recommended to use a glass or ceramic container, as metal containers can react with the acidic nature of the starter. Mix the flour and water until well combined, making sure there are no dry pockets of flour. Cover the container loosely with a clean cloth or plastic wrap, allowing air to circulate.

Now comes the waiting game. Place the container in a warm spot, ideally around 70-75°F (21-24°C). The warmth helps to activate the natural yeast and bacteria present in the flour. Over the next few days, you will begin to see signs of fermentation. Bubbles will start to form on the surface, indicating that the yeast is becoming active. You may also notice a slightly sour smell, which is a good sign that the fermentation process is underway.

During the first few days, it is important to feed your sourdough starter regularly. This involves discarding a portion of the starter and replenishing it with fresh flour and water. By removing a portion of the starter, you are preventing it from becoming too acidic and maintaining a healthy balance of yeast and bacteria. The discarded portion can be used in other recipes, such as pancakes or waffles, or simply discarded.

To feed your sourdough starter, remove about half of the starter from the container and discard it. Then, add equal parts of flour and water to the remaining starter, stirring until well combined. This feeding process should be repeated every 12-24 hours, depending on the activity of your starter. If your starter is very active and bubbling vigorously, it may need to be fed more frequently.

As your sourdough starter matures, it will become stronger and more active. This process can take anywhere from a few days to a couple of weeks, depending on various factors such as temperature and the type of flour used. You will know that your starter is ready to use when it consistently doubles in size within a few hours of feeding and has a pleasant, tangy aroma."

"The Delicate Nature of Pastry Breads: Pastry breads are a unique and delicate type of baked goods that require special attention and care during the baking process. These breads are known for their light and flaky texture, which is achieved through a combination of precise measurements, specific ingredients, and careful handling techniques.

One of the key factors that contribute to the delicate nature of pastry breads is the use of a high-fat content in the dough. This fat, usually in the form of butter or shortening, is what creates the layers and flakiness in the bread. However, it also means that the dough is more prone to melting or becoming greasy if not handled properly. This is why it is crucial to keep the dough and all the ingredients cold throughout the entire process.

Another important aspect of making pastry breads is the technique used to incorporate the fat into the dough. This is typically done through a process called ""laminating,"" which involves folding and rolling the dough multiple times to create layers. Each time the dough is rolled, the fat is spread evenly, resulting in a flaky texture. However, it is essential to be gentle and avoid overworking the dough, as this can lead to tough and dense bread.

In addition to the fat content and laminating technique, the type of flour used also plays a significant role in the delicate nature of pastry breads. Pastry flour, which has a lower protein content compared to all-purpose flour, is often preferred for these breads. The lower protein content helps to create a more tender and delicate crumb, which is desired in pastry breads. It is important to note that using the right type of flour is crucial for achieving the desired texture and structure in the final product.

Furthermore, the baking process itself requires careful attention to detail. Pastry breads are typically baked at a higher temperature than other types of bread to ensure that the fat in the dough melts and creates steam, which helps to create the flaky layers. However, it is crucial to monitor the baking time closely, as overbaking can result in dry and tough bread. It is recommended to use a thermometer to check the internal temperature of the bread to ensure it is fully cooked but not overdone.

Overall, the delicate nature of pastry breads requires precision, patience, and attention to detail. From the selection of ingredients to the handling and baking process, every step must be carefully executed to achieve the desired light and flaky texture."

"Understanding Yeast and Its Role in Bread Baking: Yeast is a single-celled microorganism that plays a crucial role in bread baking. It belongs to the fungi kingdom and is commonly used as a leavening agent in the production of bread and other baked goods. Yeast is responsible for the fermentation process, which is essential for the development of the dough and the final texture and flavor of the bread.

In bread baking, yeast converts the sugars present in the dough into carbon dioxide gas and alcohol through a process called fermentation. This gas is what causes the dough to rise and gives bread its light and airy texture. The alcohol produced during fermentation evaporates during the baking process, leaving behind the distinct aroma and flavor associated with freshly baked bread.

There are two main types of yeast used in bread baking: active dry yeast and instant yeast. Active dry yeast is the most commonly used type and is typically sold in small granules or pellets. It needs to be activated by dissolving it in warm water before adding it to the dough. Instant yeast, on the other hand, is a more finely ground form of yeast that can be added directly to the dry ingredients without the need for activation.

The ideal temperature for yeast to thrive and ferment is between 75°F and 85°F (24°C and 29°C). At this temperature range, yeast activity is at its peak, and the fermentation process occurs at an optimal rate. If the temperature is too low, yeast activity slows down, resulting in a longer rise time. Conversely, if the temperature is too high, yeast can become overactive and produce an undesirable flavor in the bread.

To ensure the yeast is active and alive, it is often proofed before being added to the dough. Proofing involves dissolving the yeast in warm water with a small amount of sugar and allowing it to sit for a few minutes. If the yeast is active, it will start to foam and bubble, indicating that it is ready to be used. If there is no foaming or bubbling, it means the yeast is inactive or expired and should be discarded.

In addition to its leavening properties, yeast also contributes to the flavor and aroma of bread. During fermentation, yeast produces various compounds, including organic acids and volatile compounds, which give bread its characteristic taste and smell. These compounds interact with other ingredients in the dough, such as sugars and proteins, to create a complex and unique flavor profile.

It is important to handle yeast properly to ensure optimal bread baking results. Yeast should be stored"

INSTEAD OF PROLOGUE

I always think about one thing – why meals cooked by following the same recipe and with using same ingredients can be so different?

Why for one person cooking bread is easy like piece of cake, but for another one this process seems to be so time consuming that his decision not to do it at all, and third person have a desire and don't afraid of difficulties, but nothing is working.

I decide to find out why this happens.

And, how it develops, the main role in achievement of desirable result is playing not skills, ambitions or absence of abilities, but, first of all, lack of knowledge.

Sometimes it is very difficult to cook with different cookbooks especially at first, since the recipes have only cooking time, list of ingredients and the instructions how to peel, wash and boil or roast them.

However, for young people who don't prepared and couldn't determine what is missing in that recipe and how to fill the missing links to make as result wonderful meal, it is hard to start cooking according to these recipes.

The complexity is also containing in that they are not chefs and they don't have enough knowledge or qualification, but they want to cook good for their family and themselves, they want to know how to bake bread and surprise their relatives and folks with delicious dinner or supper.

WHAT TO DO TO MAKE THE COOKING PROCESS UNDERSTANDABLE FOR EVERYONE?

The answer is pretty simple: we will need to particularly describe all cooking steps to make them clearly understandable for which purposes we do this operation, what we need to avoid and why.

Unfortunately, many cookbooks ignore these details in two reasons: they think that it is too simple and don't have need to mention or because of lack of knowledge.

Of course, if this book was written for professional, many detailed steps can be skipped, but if it is for everyone, it will need explanations, especially when not all people could understand that.

For example, what will be, if you fry onion on the high heat or what will become with dough if you will leave it for overtime? This knowledge you can get from the method of tests and mistakes or from cookbooks, where you will find more detailed guidance.

Once I shared one of my recipes with my friend, where I wrote that the onion should be cooked on the low heat until it become transparent. Then you should slightly season it with salt and drizzle with a splash of rice vinegar or lemon juice and continue cooking on the low heat. When my friend's husband starts to cook this dish according to the recipe, he asked why all these steps are required and why you couldn't skip that and just fry onion. And then I realized that it is not enough to share only the knowledge with other people, but it is also quite important to correctly explain to make it understandable for which reason and why you do that.

Of course, for one recipe you should stir – fry onion on the high heat to make it caramelized faster. But in previous case onion should be cooked on very low heat because that will make it transparent and with light taste and smooth texture. And if you drizzle it with a splash of rice vinegar or lemon juice, onion will gain a nice pleasant aroma and velvety flavor.

According to this we can come to conclusion that it is important to know not only the recipe but also the cooking technology. That is why all recipes should be thoroughly considered and repeatedly tested and particularly explained.

For example, you could know various fine details like that bread buns will turn out better on thin aluminum baking sheet than on regular baking tray because second one preferable to use for such meals which requires more than 20 minutes. Also baking tray is perfect if you want to treat your family with freshly baked sweet buns or pies.

I often use thin aluminum baking sheets for sweet cookies, especially because they become crispy and it helps to prevent them from burning as well.

However, we distracted a little bit so let's return to baking bread.

In this culinary book we will learn such useful things as:
- How to make sourdough starter and how to work with it
- How to cook sourdough bread with small amount of yeast or without them
- How to make dough with yeast and other flavorings
- How to cook bread
- How to make simple and delicious pastry, sweet cakes, pies and buns

Also, our book is included various bread recipes, special techniques and helpful tips.

PROFESSOR RAYMOND CALVEL
AND HIS METHOD

Since we are writing the book of making bread, we couldn't not to mention the famous expert in this area. Thanks to him, were invented different forms and methods of baking bread which still using in bakeries around the world.

Well – known professor of bread making Raymond Calvel was French baker. He devoted all his life to this work, compare different types of flour and influence of ingredients with end product.

He baked bread and taught others how to do it properly. Wonderful Julia Child and her friend and co-author Simone Beck studied the art of baking traditional French bread from professor Calvel and received knowledge became the base of one of the chapters of book "Master the art of French cuisine".

The professor's book "Le Goût du Pain", also known as "Taste of Bread", was brilliant ending of his career and it became real treasure for those people who wanted or want to learn how to bake delicious homemade bread.

THE INFLUENCE OF INGREDIENTS ON BREAD

According to the old legend the process of making bread with sourdough was invented accidentally. One housewife prepared dough with water and flour and left it for long time. Because of inattention it began to ferment and as result doubled in size. The woman arrived at an idea to cook bread with leaven dough. And that's how was born the method of making sourdough.

Therefore, each ingredient can have influence with cooking process, taste and texture of bread.

For example, when you mix water with flour, starch and proteins start to absorb liquid and transform into gluten creating a strong connection between each other. Thanks to that, structure of bread gets thick and spongy.

Salt also play significant role in baking of bread. It is taking part in creation of good taste and pleasant aroma of end product. It is important to mention that salt is an antioxidant which helps bread to stay fresh longer.

Yeast and sourdough starter have specific influence with making process. However, sourdough certainly has a few advantages.

First of all, thank to it bread have nice deep flavor, rich texture and firm accurate form.

Secondly, sourdough bread is healthier than yeast one since sourdough is natural product which produce by hand (even though there are exist some kinds of machine production).

Lastly, bread with sourdough keeps longer than regular one.

Sourdough is one of the oldest inventions of humankind. The first mention of it date about 3000 years before Christ.

This method of fermentation is containing that dough from wheat or rye flour leaven with mixed culture, which consist of natural wild yeast and lactic acid bacteria.

Baker make sourdough starter during several days (about 3 to 5 usually) before making bread. Its basic components are 50 % of wheat flour, 50 % of rye flour and 50 % of liquid from the amount of flour. For sourdough you can use various sweet juices especially from apple or grape, potato stock, raisins, honey and yogurt.

METHOD OF MAKING SOURDOUGH STARTER WITH WHEAT AND RYE FLOUR

You can make sourdough starter with only wheat or rye flour. But according to method of famous French professor of bread making Raymond Calvel it is better to use the mix of two types of flour.

Ingredients:

300 gr. wheat flour
300 gr. rye flour
3 gr. malt
3 gr. fine sea salt
360 gr. water

Directions:

1. Mix all ingredients into dough until combine, cover it with plastic wrap and set aside in warm place at 27 °C (81 °F) for 22 hours. Then discard one half of doughy mixture or share it with friends. Add 300 grams of flour, 180 grams of water, 1 gram of salt and 2 grams of malt. Set aside for 7 hours, then repeat this process but without adding malt.

2. When sourdough will stand for 7 hours, repeat the process for 3 times with resting time for about 6 hours each time. During it ripeness sourdough will increase in volume and that is why each time we will throw away one half. After 54 hours (about 2 with half days) sourdough will be ready to use.

To refresh use the following method:

1. For 520 grams of prepared sourdough we will need 675 grams of flour and 405 grams of water. Mix all ingredients with stand mixer on the low speed for 10 minutes until it become smooth and elastic. Cover it with plastic wrap and set aside for 5 to 6 hours at 27 °C (81 °F).

2. It is also recommended keep sourdough in refrigerator at 10° C (50 °F).

3. Further in this book we will thoroughly learn about all steps of making bread and different terms such as sourdough starter, autolyze and pre – ferment (also known as sponge or pre – dough).

TIPS:

Check the metric conversion chart in the end of this book.

METHOD OF AUTOLYSE OF
PROFESSOR RAYMOND CALVEL

In our book there are a lot of recipes including this method. However, firstly we need to know about it and why it is needed.

Autolyse is process of pre kneading dough from all flour and water which are required for recipe.

According to Raymond Calvel's experiments autolyse is improving the texture of bread and connections between starch, gluten and water.

As result, when you make second kneading and add the remaining ingredients (sourdough, salt, spices, seeds and etc.), dough become smooth and elastic faster, and after baking bread will gain nice spongy texture. For the most part this method is used for sourdough bread.

PROFESSOR RAYMOND CALVEL'S
RYE AND WHEAT BREAD

As the base we will use the professor's method, but we will make few changes and add some ingredients to elevate the flavor of our bread.

Before you start to make this bead, thoroughly read the recipe and process of making, prepare all necessary ingredients and calculate cooking time for sourdough and bread.

If you will cope with each step the result won't let you wait for it. All of your efforts seasoned with creative approach will be defensible and you will gain delicious wonderful aromatic and healthy bread.

Ingredients:

1714 gr. flour
40 gr. salt
20 gr. fresh yeast
1105, 8 gr. water
530 gr. pre – ferment (sponge)
40 gr. malt syrup
10 gr. pumpkin seeds
8 gr. sesame seeds
8 gr. linen seeds
8 gr. oat flakes

For pre - ferment:

72 gr. sourdough starter
285, 5 gr. flour
171, 5 gr water

Directions:

Pre – ferment or sponge:

1. Mix sourdough starter, flour and water with stand mixer on the low speed for 10 minutes. Cover with plastic wrap and set aside for 5 to 6 hours 24 °C/ 76 °F. After that pre – ferment (sponge) will be ready to use.

Autolyse:

2. Add 1714 grams of flour and 1105, 8 grams of water into mixer and knead on the low speed for 5 minutes, cover mixing bowl with plastic wrap and set aside for 30 minutes.

Method of making bread:

3. In autolyse add pre – ferment, seeds, malt syrup (sometimes I change it to glucose syrup or organic honey), increase the speed and knead dough with stand mixer for 10 minutes. Cover it with plastic wrap and set aside for 45 minutes.

4. Put dough on table dusted with some flour. Sprinkle linen cloth with flour and start kneading dough for several minutes. Divide it into pieces and roll them into balls. Set aside for 35 minutes. We will make baguettes and one big bread. Shape balls into bread, transfer to linen cloth, cover with clean kitchen cloth and set aside for 2 hours.

5. Preheat oven to 230 °C /446 °F. Make cuts, grease bread with water and sprinkle with seeds and oat flakes and bake into oven for 25 to 40 minutes depends of your oven type. Completely cool before serving.

TIPS:

Before baking bread, I always spray oven with water to create steam.

WHAT WE WILL NEED TO START MAKING BREAD AND WHAT IS IMPORTANT TO KNOW ABOUT IT?

1. First of all, we will need fresh sourdough starter and small amount of yeast – about 2 to 3 grams for each 500 – 600 grams of dough.

2. If you make bread with yeast it is better to use fresh pressed yeast, but you can use active dry yeast as well. However, before using both types of yeast you should check them if they are good enough.

3. I often make pre – ferment (pre-dough or also known as sponge) with yeast. There are two kinds of pre-ferment: sponge (with yeast) and sourdough (without yeasts). We will make first one. For this you will need long jug. Mix together in jug warm water, 1 teaspoon of sugar, 1 tablespoon of flour and yeast and set aside in warm place. This process is important to understand are yeast active or not. It they won't rise dough will become flat.

Thereafter you could not do the pre – ferment especially if you confident about your yeast, but in first time I recommend you repeat all process to the end.

4. If it is cool into your home, water will become cold faster and fermentation process will not happen. However, we can easily figure it out. Bring to the boil water in kettle. Prepare yeast mixture, put into microwave and next to it glass with hot water, but does not turn on the microwave. Close the door and let it sit for several minutes.

After couple minutes fermentation process will start and yeast will rise. If it will not happen that means yeast is not working. You should buy another one and start all over again, because if yeast is bad, bread won't turn out great.

5. Before you start to make the dough, it is recommended sift flour to rich it with oxygen and remove any lumps.

6. You should add liquid according to how much do you add into pre-ferment sponge. Also, instead of water you could add milk, sour cream, buttermilk or sometimes juice.

7. Almost any type of oil is suitable for dough. If you cook regular bread oil will not be necessary.

TECHNOLOGY OF MAKING BREAD

Make the pre-ferment or sponge as it was written before. After when pre-ferment will be ready, add remaining liquid and mix well. Sift flour with salt, add ground spices, fried onion (if you made onion bread), olives and seeds. Give a good stir and combine liquid with dry ingredients. Knead the dough until it become smooth and elastic. If you think that is not enough flour, add a little bit because too much flour will make bread crumbly and dry.

Knead the dough until it easily sticks out from the sides of bowl.

If you make dough but there are no scales on hand, do not worry, combine spices and all additions to liquid and then add flour little by little. Gradually add flour with one hand and use another one to knead dough with circular clockwise motions.

Regulate amount of flour until dough start to easily stick out from your hands. Shape dough into ball, put in clean and dry bowl, cover with linen cloth and set aside in warm place. You can speed up this process by using method with microwave (as it was written before). Also, you could slightly grease bowl with thin layer of olive oil before you put the dough. It will help dough easily come out from the sides of bowl when it is doubles in size.

A BIT OF CLASSIFICATION

There are two types of products which make with flour: bread and pastry.

The main difference is that in bread the most important ingredient is flour. However, in pastry flour just a part of mixture which content butter (or oil), sugar, dairy free milk, eggs (if you use them) and other various additions.

HEALTHY SOURDOUGH BREAD

WHAT IS SOURDOUGH AND HOW TO MAKE IT

Sourdough is a natural product produced from wheat flour mixed with water and small amount of sweetener (usually it is a honey, but you could replace it sugar).

Instead of water sometimes I take prepared in advance fruit infusion. It is very easy to make it. Slice an apple into pieces (I recommend to buy sweet kinds of apples), put into a bowl or jug, add a little bit of washed and drained raisin, pinch of sugar and warm water. Cover and set aside in warm dry place at room temperature for several days. After that strain water through a sieve and discard apple and raisin. Now you can use this fruit infusion for making sourdough starter.

Trust me, this is totally worth it. In the end as result bread will have slightly sweet aroma and velvety smooth taste.

During the fermentation process sourdough starter start to produce useful lactic acid bacteria and thanks to it bread have such airy and soft texture. Also, it is good to know that sourdough bread keeps longer than regular one.

Contrary to popular opinion, the sourdough starter is very easy to make. And now we are going to learn how.

HOW TO MAKE SIMPLE SOURDOUGH STARTER?

First of all, we will 100 grams of flour, 100 grams of water and couple teaspoons of honey (you can replace it with sugar).

You can use wheat or rye flour depends of what type of sourdough starter you want to get.

In separate plastic container mix water with flour and honey or sugar until combine (make sure that there are no lumps in mixture). Cover with plastic lid and keep in warm and dry place for 12 hours.

Then you should "feed up" the sourdough starter. For example, if you made it at 8 AM, you should feed it at 8 PM. When the feeding time has come, discard 100 grams of starter and add 100 grams of flour, 100 grams of water and some sugar or honey.

Why it is necessary to throw out some sourdough starter?

Everything is pretty simple – we won't need a huge amount of sourdough starter in the end. To activate the starter, it should ripen for 5 to 6 days and during this period we need to feed it once each 12 hours. That's why we discard excess sourdough starter. However, you can share it with your friends or folks.

After first feeding you can use the fruit infusion, the recipe we will wrote above.

When the sourdough starter will ripen, you should "block" it – put in fridge for 1 day. Then you can feed it once per 24 hours. It is highly recommended to not to skip the feeding time more than for 2 days. Otherwise starter will lose its power.

HOW TO REFRESH SOURDOUGH STARTER?

If you didn't feed the sourdough starter more than 2 day due to some reasons, don't worry, you can reanimate it.

For that you should feed the starter and leave it at room temperature for one day. Then, feed it once more and keep it at room temperature for one day more. After two day the sourdough starter will rehabilitate, and you can use it for baking bread. Also, you could dry the sourdough starter and it will help to keep it for longer time.

Prepared sourdough starter should have good smell, thick consistency and not sweet and not sour taste. You can put a little bit of yeasts together with sourdough starter to make it stronger and help bread to rise.

However, you could use only sourdough starter and it will make your bread healthier and more nutritious.

AUTOLYSE

As we mention before, this method was invented by French baker expert Raymond Calvel, author of famous "Le Goût du Pain" also known as "Taste of Bread".

Autolyse is a process of making dough start from mix of flour and water. Then it leaves in warm place for 1 hour before you add remaining ingredients (sourdough starter, salt, spices and other additions: nuts, olives, chocolate, raisins and etc.). After that time, you can easily work with dough and it get nice special texture.

Bread cooked according this method have precise aroma, wonderful taste and tender spongy texture.

I could spend time describing how much I like sourdough bread. What a wonderful aroma this bread has! It reminds me warm and cozy home and lovely family evenings with homemade food and pastry.

I want to share it with you my dear readers. Hope you will have wonderful time reading this book and cooking with my recipes.

Have a wonderful tasty day like my sourdough bread!

Alright, let's make some delicious bread!

CACAO SOURDOUGH BREAD WITH RAISINS

Today we will make aromatic and freshly baked homemade bread with cacao and raisins, crunchy outside and very soft and tender inside.

Its scent often reminds me my childhood when my mother baked homemade bread, various pastries at weekends, folks and neighbors came together. It was our specific tradition – invite everyone to us for treats. We listened to nice music, conversed, played games, sometimes danced, enjoyed herbal fragrant tea and spent wonderful time.

Now I grew up, I have my own children and I teach them how to cook and bake. Traditions should be handed down from generation to generation, keeping the family heritage, homey coziness and time, when you still wanted to be that small child who woke up from scent of freshly baked bread and mother's: "Good morning, my sun".

My mother is no longer with us, but this wonderful aroma of fresh bread still reminds me my childhood memories when she was by me and I feel her love as before.

Cook with pleasure and love for your family, as the years have been passed leaving in unconscious our precious memories and dream, which after time you will appreciate more and more.

This bread you can cook in two ways. The first way will be with autolyse, other will be without the autolyse but in same consistency. After that we will make village bread without autolyse.

Ingredients:

For liquid mixture with cocoa:

23 gr. cocoa powder
60 gr. warm water
15 gr. brown cane sugar
½ tsp. cinnamon
2 gr. cardamom

For autolyse:

560 gr. bread flour
280 gr. water
90 gr. liquid cocoa mixture
2 – 2.5 gr. active dry yeast

For final kneading:

60 gr. wheat sourdough starter
12 gr. salt
80 gr. dried fruits, sliced into small cubes
14 gr. raisins

Directions:

1. First of all, we need to sift cocoa powder, add spices, brown sugar, water and stir until combine.

2. After that, make the autolyse with prepared liquid mixture. If we use stand mixer for making dough, add all ingredients for autolyse into mixing bowl and start preparing the dough on the low speed for 5 to 7 minutes. Then cover mixing bowl with plastic wrap and put autolyse in warm place for 1 to 2 hours.

3. Then combine autolyse with salt and sourdough starter in mixer and mix on the low speed for 5 minutes, and then 5 minutes more on high speed.

4. Dust the working surface with some flour and knead prepared dough for several minutes, shape it into a ball and put into a bowl, cover with plastic wrap and set aside for 1 to 1 ½ hour.

5. In this bread you can also add some seeds, nuts, dried fruits or chocolate chips. You should add them after you mix dough with sourdough starter and salt. For this recipe we will need 95 – 100 grams of chopped dried apricots and raisins.

6. Thereafter dough has rested at room temperature, put it into fridge for 12 to 16 hours. That is needed to help dough activate the gluten and create such chewy spongy texture. The temperature in fridge should be 4 to 5 °C / 39,2 – 41 °F.

7. Sprinkle the working surface or cutting board with some flour. Transfer dough to cutting board and shape it a ball. If you want to make buns, divide dough into small pieces and form balls.

8. Cover dough with plastic wrap and let it sit for another 30 minutes. Dust thick linen cloth with some flour and put dough on it. If you don't have thick linen cloth, put prepared dough on a tray lined with baking paper. Cover with plastic wrap or kitchen cloth and let it rise for several minutes.

9. Take a blade and make some cuts on top of the bread. Preheat oven to 220 – 230 °C / 428 – 446 °F. Don't forget to spray oven with water to create a steam.

10. Reduce the heat to 180 °C / 356 °F. The baking time depends of size of your bread and your oven, approximately 25 to 40 minutes. But, of course, it is better to be closer to your oven and keep an eye on bread to not burn it. Check the doneness with wooden stick – if it's comes out dry and clean that means bread is ready.

11. Cool bread on the wire rack and slice it.

TIPS:

Also, you can use special bread baskets to help it rise even more easily and quickly. If you buy them in special shop for bakers, they should have linen or cotton cover. Don't forget to dust them with some flour and semolina mixture before putting bread.

FRENCH VILLAGE SOURDOUGH BREAD

It is easy to understand that I am a fan of making bread. This unforgettable process of creating something special that reminds you a coziness and warmth or home. Every single piece, each bite is so delicate, but in the same time chewy with rich flavor and soft spongy texture.

Bread can be versatile. You have like a clean canvas and free-range space for experiments, creativity and emotions.

Each of my recipes tells its own story. It is not just a combination of flavors and ingredients. All of them have their own characteristics, taste, aroma and shape. And the most exciting thing that you can make bread as you like: twisted, braided, buns, big or small and etc. However, we should not overdo with bread. Try to eat it periodically, in small portions and it will be fine.

Ingredients:

100 gr. wheat sourdough starter
350 gr. wheat flour
100 gr. village flour
70 gr. rye flour
½ tbsp. sugar
12 gr. salt
3 gr. active dry yeast
1 tbsp. dairy free milk
340 gr. water

Directions:

1. For making dough take the warm water about 23 – 30 °C / 73,4 – 86 °F. Add sourdough starter (same temperature), sugar, salt, yeast and sifted flour, mix well. If you use a stand mixer, prepare dough on the low speed for 2 to 3 minutes. Scrape dough from the bottom and sides of your mixing bowl, knead it a little bit by hands and mix with mixer on the high speed for another 2 to 3 minutes.

2. Transfer dough to working surface dusted with some flour, knead it for couple minutes and shape into a ball, put into mixing bowl and cover with plastic wrap. Keep in warm place for 1 to 2 hours and then put in fridge for 12 to 18 hours.

3. Sprinkle large cutting board with flour, put the dough and knead it for several minutes, divide into 2 pieces, make balls and cover with clean cloth and let it rise for 1 to 2 hours. Mix 2 – 3 tablespoons of flour with same amount of semolina and dust a thick linen cloth with prepared mixture. It will help bread to not stick to linen.

4. Shape the dough into round, put on prepared dusted cloth, make crosswise cuts, sprinkle with oat flakes and set aside for 35 to 40 minutes. Carefully transfer bread to baking sheet or tray lined with baking paper and dusted with some semolina and flour mixture.

5. Preheat oven to 220° C / 428 °F. Spray oven and bread with some water.

6. Put bread into oven for 10 minutes, then reduce the heat to 180 °C / 356 °F and bake for another 20 – 30 minutes depends of your oven's type until it become nice and crispy golden.

TIPS:

Check the readiness of bread with wooden stick or knock on the bottom of bread. You should hear loud sound.

OAT & WHEAT SOURDOUGH BREAD

In early morning, far away from noisy cities, with lovely songs of birds and amazing aroma of wild flowers let's relax and bake wonderful spongy bread made with oats and natural homemade sourdough.

Serve it with cup of hot chocolate, salted caramel sauce or your favorite jam. Smell this delicious aroma of freshly baked bread and enjoy every moment in your life.

Ingredients:

For autolyse:

198 gr. oat flour
367 gr. wheat flour
320 gr. water

For second kneading:

113 gr. wheat sourdough starter
11 gr. salt
2,5 gr. active dry yeast

For garnish:

Sesame seeds
Oat flakes
Pumpkin seeds
Linen seeds

Directions:

Autolyse:

1. Sift wheat flour into mixing bowl and add the remaining ingredients. Mix on the low speed for 5 to 7 minutes, cover with plastic wrap and keep in warm and dry place for 2 hours.

Second kneading:

2. Add all ingredients for second batch in dough and mix firstly on the low speed then on the high speed for 5 minutes. The temperature of dough should be about 23 °C /74,3 °F.

3. Cover it with plastic wrap and leave at room temperature for 30 minutes. Put dough in fridge for 12 to 18 hours. The temperature in fridge should be not more than 5 °C / 41 °F.

4. Dust working surface with flour, put the dough on top and knead for couple minutes, divide it into pieces, cover with clean cloth and let it sit for 40 minutes.

5. Transfer bread to thick linen cloth dusted with some flour and semolina and set aside until it doubles in size.

6. Preheat oven to 230° C / 446 °F. Make cuts on top of the bread, spray with some water and sprinkle with sesame seeds, pumpkin seeds, linen seeds and oat flakes.
Put bread into oven and reduce the heat to 220° C / 428 °F. Bake until nice golden color.

BUCKWHEAT GRAIN BREAD WITH PUMPKIN SEEDS

Buckwheat bread is not only tasty but also very healthy product for our organism. It is rich of vitamins B, A and E, such minerals like calcium, zinc, potassium and sodium. This bread made from buckwheat flour and that is why it becomes very nutritious with nice nutty flavor and thick spongy texture.

At times you need to give a rest for your organism and eat something simple and healthy like buckwheat sourdough grain bread with pumpkin seeds.

Why with sourdough starter? – You may ask, and I will answer that the sourdough bread is the one of healthiest type of food. And it is not so hard to make it as many people think.

Let's talk a little bit about sourdough starter. What is it? As we wrote before, sourdough starter is a thing which is preparing on the base of flour. It contains useful lactic acid bacteria which helps bread to have a nice soft spongy texture. You can make various bread and pastry with sourdough starter. But firstly, it needs to ripen and that is why the process of making it takes enough time. Also, sourdough bread positively affects not only on our stomach but also on whole body.

Ingredients:

415 gr. wheat flour
105 gr. buckwheat flour
105 gr. wheat sourdough starter
10 gr. salt
2,5 gr. fresh yeast
50 gr. pumpkin seeds
365 gr. water

Directions:

1. Toast 70% of pumpkin seeds in a frying pan and completely cool. Sift wheat flour into mixing bowl, add toasted pumpkin seeds and buckwheat flour, wheat sourdough starter, warm water about 23 – 30° C / 74,3 – 86 °F, yeast and salt. Mix with mixer for 2 to 3 minutes on the low speed. Scrape the dough from sides, knead it a little bit with your hands and mix for 2 to 3 minutes more on the high speed. Put the dough into a bowl, cover with plastic wrap and keep in warm place for 1 to 3 hours, and then put in fridge for 12 – 18 hours.

2. Dust the working surface with flour and knead dough for couple minutes, shape it into ball and cut in two pieces. Make balls again and cover with clean cloth, set aside for 1 to 2 hours.

3. Combine 3 tablespoons of flour with same amount of semolina and sprinkle it on top of thick linen cloth. Shape one piece of dough into rectangle a little bit smaller than a baking pan. Line baking pans with baking paper and dust them with some semolina and flour mixture. Put dough into pans, make some crosswise cuts, sprinkle with pumpkin seeds on top and leave it rest for another 35 to 40 minutes.

4. Preheat oven to 220°C / 428 °F. Spray it and bread with some water. Bake bread for 10 minutes, then reduce heat to 170°C /338 °F and bake for 25 – 30 minutes more until nice golden.

TIPS:

For this recipe you can use a ground buckwheat or buckwheat flour.

Check the readiness with wooden stick – if it comes out easy and clean, bread is ready

BRAN SOURDOUGH BREAD

Not so long ago white soft bread was considered as highly nutritious and healthy product. It was produced from wheat flour, big amount of sugar, yeast and butter. And brans were utilized as useless thing.

Now many people think that bran bread is one of the healthiest kinds of bread. But why?

First of all, let's discuss what are brans and why they good for our body. Brans are protective shell of wheat grain. They contain useful minerals, iron, pectin, cellulose and vitamins B1, E, C and D. Bran bread is a storehouse of healthy attributes for organism. It helps to normalize the metabolism, improve the microflora of intestine and rising of immunity.

This type of bread is a dietetic product which practically not contains bad fats and carbohydrates. That's why you could enjoy each piece of freshly baked bran bread without thinking about your figure or weight. But, don't overdo with it.

Ingredients:

277 gr. wheat sourdough starter
740 gr. wheat flour or whole-wheat flour
355 gr. brans
260 gr. plant-based milk (about 38 ˚C)
380 gr. warm water
11 gr. salt
2,5 – 3 gr. yeast
7 gr. sugar, syrup or honey

Directions:

1. Combine all dry ingredients in mixing bowl. In a jug add all liquid and mix well, pour in dry mixture and give a good stir with spatula. Knead dough with stand mixer for 5 minutes on the low speed and then 5 to 10 minutes on the high speed. Dough temperature should be around 25 °C/ 77 °F.

2. Cover with plastic wrap and set aside in warm place for 1 hour.

Knead dough by your hands, cover with plastic wrap and put in fridge for 12 to 18 hours. The temperature of fridge should be not more than 3 – 5 °C/ 37,4 – 41 °F.

3. Dust working surface with some flour, put the dough on top and divide into pieces. Shape them into balls, cover with clean cloth and set aside for 30 to 45 minutes. Form bread and transfer to thick linen cloth. Don't forget to sprinkle it with semolina and flour mixture. Cover with kitchen towel or plastic wrap and let it rest for 30 minutes.

4. Carefully transfer dough to lined baking tray, previously dusted with some flour and semolina. Make crosswise cuts with blade or razor.

5. Preheat oven to 230° C/ 446 °F. Then low the temperature to 220° C /428 °F. Spay the oven with some water to create steam and bake bread until nice golden color.

TIPS:

Baking time depends of your oven type, its abilities and also of bread size. Check the readiness with wooden stick.

PUMPKIN SOURDOUGH BREAD

The healthiest favorite vegetable during the autumn season is pumpkin. You can cook a lot of meals with it staring from Italian ravioli pasta to famous American pumpkin pie.

But, as I think, there is nothing better than Pumpkin bread. Soft and aromatic inside and crispy outside – this bread is perfect for breakfast, lunch, dinner or fast snack. You can use it for delicious and nutritious sandwiches, toasts or just enjoy a slice of fresh bread with coffee or tea.

As an addition we used toasted pumpkin seeds for garnish, but you can easily replace them with other seeds or oat flakes. Before eating this bread, it has to be chilled. That will help it to get thick texture and rich taste.

Ingredients:

113 gr. wheat sourdough starter
520 gr. wheat flour
½ tbsp. sugar
100 gr. pumpkin puree
15 gr. toasted pumpkin seeds
12 gr. fine sea salt
2 to 3 gr. yeast
300 gr. water

For garnish:

Toasted pumpkin seeds

Directions:

1. For making dough take warm water 23 – 30 °C /73,4 – 86 °F, add pumpkin puree and wheat sourdough starter with the same temperature, salt, sugar, yeast, sifted flour and mix well until combine. If you use stand mixer, knead the dough firstly on low speed for 2 to 3 minutes. Scrape mixture from the sides of mixing bowl, increase speed and keep kneading dough for 2 – 3 minutes.

2. Cover dough with plastic wrap and set aside in warm place for 1,5 to 3 hours. After, keep dough in fridge for 12 – 18 hours.

Put dough on flat working surface dusted with some flour and cut it in two pieces, shape into balls, cover with kitchen towel and set aside for 1 – 2 hours.

3. Mix 2 to 3 tablespoons of flour with same amount of semolina.

Shape dough into rectangle, transfer to thick linen cloth and make some cuts. Set aside for 35 to 40 minutes. Put bread into baking pan previously lined with baking paper and dusted with flour and semolina mixture.

4. Preheat oven to 220 °C / 428 °F, spray it and bread with some water.

Sprinkle bread with toasted pumpkin seeds and bake into oven for 10 minutes, then reduce heat to 180 °C / 356 °F and bake for 20 – 30 minutes more. Baking time depends of your oven type. For example, if you have gas oven it will take longer to bake bread, much more than 15 or 20 minutes. Check the readiness of bread with wooden stick or you can knock on the bottom of bread and if you hear a loud sound, bread is ready.

TIPS:

Also, you can put shaped dough in special bread baskets. I suggest you to buy it round or rectangle shape. If you buy it in specialized bakery shop, you should pay attention to that basket should be lined with thick cotton or linen cloth. But if you bought basket without linen case, you can sew it by yourself or just simply line basket with linen cloth. Dust it with some semolina, put dough inside and set aside for 30 to 35 minutes.

RYE SOURDOUGH BREAD

Rye sourdough bread is one of our favorite. Despite that it takes a bit of time to make it, the final result and benefits are licking all creation.

Rye bread is fewer calories than products cooked from wheat flour. It contains big amount of vitamins and amino acids. Also, this bread is great source of cellulose (a polysaccharide that is the chief constituent of all plant tissues and fibers), one of the most important things for our stomach and especially for intestine.

The big advantage of rye bread that it keeps longer than regular wheat one and that is why I like to use it for avocado breakfast sandwiches with fresh tomatoes or PB & J. You can simply take them away with you to your work, school or even as snack for small picnic.

Ingredients:

300 gr. dark rye flour
200 gr. whole meal wheat flour
335 gr. water
25 gr. sesame seeds
20 gr. linen seeds
25 gr. sunflower seeds
100 gr. wheat sourdough starter
11,5 gr. salt
2,5 gr. yeast
1 tbsp. sugar

For sprinkling:

Sesame seeds or semolina

Directions:

1. Toast all seeds and completely cool at room temperature. Add all ingredients into mixing bowl and knead the dough in stand mixer first at low speed for 3 minutes, then at high speed for 5 minutes more.

2. The dough temperature should be around 23° C / 73,4 °F. Cover dough with plastic wrap and put in fridge for 12 – 18 hours.

3. Dust the working surface with some flour. Put dough to working surface, knead it a little bit and cut into pieces. Shape them into bread, cover with kitchen cloth and set aside for 40 minutes. Transfer bread to thick linen cloth.

4. Preheat oven to 230° C / 446 °F, thoroughly spray it with water. Make some cuts on top of bread surface with sharp blade or knife, slightly spray it with water, sprinkle with semolina or sesame seeds and put into oven. Bake for 20 to 40 minutes at 220 °C / 428 °F.

5. The baking time depends of your oven and its abilities. Check the readiness with wooden stick or by knocking on bottom of bread. If you hear a loud sound that means bread is ready.

WHEAT AND OAT SOURDOUGH BREAD WITH OLIVES

Now there are a lot of arguments around what type of bread is healthier and is it worth to eat it. Even though the scales gradually lean towards sourdough bread, let's figure why it's like that. As we wrote before, sourdough starter is a natural product, prepared from flour, water and a little bit of sugar, syrup or even honey. Sourdough starter contain a useful lactic acid bacterium which positively effects on our body and make bread fluffy and airy. This type of bread keeps a lot longer that the regular one.

According to scientists' research sourdough bread assimilates better and contains more protein than usual white bread from supermarket. In our recipe we used whole meal wheat flour to make bread not only delicious but also healthy and nutritious. And if you add some olives and spice to dough, bread will gain an incredible aroma and taste.

Ingredients:

For autolyse:

365 gr. wheat flour
200 gr. oat flour
320 gr. water

For second kneading:

113 gr. wheat sourdough starter
11 gr. salt
2,5 gr. fresh yeast
100 gr. black olives

For sprinkling:
Sesame seeds
Oat flakes

Directions:

1. Add all ingredients for autolyse and knead dough with hook attachment at low speed for 4 to 6 minutes. Cover it with plastic wrap and set aside in warm place for 2 hours.

2. Slice black olives into small pieces. Add all ingredients into autolyse and knead dough as we did in previous recipe. Also, you could not prepare the autolyse. Just combine all dry ingredients in mixing bowl, add liquid mixture and knead it in stand mixer for 5 minutes at low speed, then 5 minutes at high speed. At the end of kneading dough temperature should be about 25 °C / 77 °F.

3. Cover it with plastic wrap and keep in warm place for 1 hour. Then knead it with your hands for some time, cover again and put in fridge for 12 to 18 hours. The fridge temperature should be not more than 3 – 5 °C / 37,4 – 41 °F.

4. Dust table or working surface with flour, put the dough on top and divide it in several pieces. Shape them into balls. Cover with clean dough and let it rest for 30 to 45 minutes. Dust thick linen cloth with some flour and semolina, shape dough in bread and cover with kitchen towel. Set aside for 30 minutes.

5. Carefully transfer bread to baking tray lined with baking paper and dusted with some semolina and flour mixture. Make cuts with blade or knife, spray with water and sprinkle with sesame seeds or oat flakes.

6. Preheat oven to 230 °C / 446 °F. Spray it with water to create steam. Bake bread into oven at 220 °C / 428 °F until nice golden color.

TIPS:

Before baking bread, dust baking pans with semolina and flour. That will help you to take out the bread a lot easier. Check the readiness with wooden stick or by knocking on bottom of bread. If you hear a loud sound that means bread is ready.

WHOLEGRAIN WHEAT BREAD WITH LINEN AND SUNFLOWER SEEDS

This old recipe often used my aunt but afterwards I improved it and make it little bit better. Bread with potato stock will be very tender with nice crispy golden crust and gorgeous aroma. Of course, before serving it is better to cool it, but this bread is too delicious so sometimes you couldn't hold down yourself and not to try a small piece.

Ingredients:

500 gr. whole - wheat flour
20 gr. linen seeds
20 gr. sunflower seeds
100 gr. wheat sourdough starter
200 gr. potato stock
11,5 gr. salt
2,5 gr. yeast
1 tbsp. sugar

Directions:

1. Toast seeds in frying pan without oil and completely cool them at room temperature.

2. Add all ingredients into mixing bowl and knead dough on low speed for 3 minutes, then increase speed to high and keep kneading for 5 minutes more. At the end of this process dough temperature should be around 23 °C / 73,4 °F.

3. Cover dough with plastic wrap and keep in warm place for 1 hour. After that knead it by hands a little bit, cover again and put in fridge for 12 to 16 hours.

4. Dust table or working surface with flour, put the dough on top and divide it in several pieces. Shape them into balls. Cover with clean dough and let it rest for 30 to 45 minutes.

5. Dust thick linen cloth with some flour and semolina, shape dough in bread and cover with kitchen towel. Set aside for 30 minutes. Carefully transfer bread to baking pan lined with baking paper and dusted with some semolina and flour mixture. Make cuts with blade or knife.

6. Preheat oven to 230 °C / 446 °F. Bake bread into oven at 220 °C / 428 °F for 15 to 20 minutes depends of your oven and its abilities. Check the readiness with wooden stick or by knocking on bottom of bread. If you hear a loud sound that means bread is ready.

TRADITIONAL SOURDOUGH BAGUETTE

French baguette is truly could be considered as one of the national symbols of France. Usually it serves for dinner or supper. This type of bread is good for sandwiches or as accompaniment for soups, salads or any other meals.

Wonderfully delicious French baguette with amazing crispy crust will be perfect as a pair for vegan cream cheese and glass of red Chardonnay.

Ingredients:

100 gr. wheat sourdough starter
450 gr. wheat flour
70 gr. bread flour
1 tbsp. sugar
11 gr. salt
3 gr. yeast
3 tbsp. olive oil
300 gr. water

Directions:

1. For preparing dough take warm water, about 25 – 30 °C / 73,4 – 86 °F. Add sourdough starter with the same temperature, sugar, salt, yeast, sifted flour and mix well. If you use stand mixer, knead dough with hook attachment for 2 to 3 minutes at low speed at first. Then, scrape dough from sides of mixing bowl, knead it a little bit with your hands and keep kneading with mixer for 5 minutes more on high speed.

2. Cover mixing bowl with plastic wrap and keep dough in warm place for 1 to 3 hours. Put the dough in fridge for 12 to 18 hours. Dust working surface with some flour, put dough on top and knead it for 5 minutes. Divide it in two parts, shape them into balls and set aside for 1 to 2 hours.

3. Combine 2 to 3 tablespoons of flour with same amount of semolina. Sprinkle a thick linen cloth with prepared dry mixture. Knead dough for several minutes, shape into baguette and transfer to sprinkled linen cloth. Make lengthwise cuts, cover with kitchen towel and set aside for 35 to 40 minutes.

4. Line the baking sheet with baking paper and sprinkle some semolina and flour mixture. Preheat oven to 220 °C / 428 °F, spray it and bread with a little bit of water.

5. Bake bread for 10 minutes, then low the temperature to 200 °C / 392 °F, spray oven with water again and bake for 15 to 20 minutes or until nice golden color. The baking time depends of your oven type.

6. Check bread for doneness with wooden stick or by knocking on bottom of bread. If you hear a loud sound that means bread is ready. Cover bread with kitchen towel and let it rest before serving.

WHEAT & RYE BREAD WITH MIXED SEEDS

The process of making fresh bread takes a lot of time but despite that I often bake at home. Since my childhood I get used to natural homemade products and so I try to cook for my family healthy but in the same time delicious meals.

Here is the recipe of tasty bread cooked from mix of rye and wheat flour. And for make it a bit fancy we will use special mixture of sesame, pumpkin, linen and sunflower seeds for garnish.

Ingredients:

300 gr. wheat flour
100 gr. rye flour
100 gr. village bread flour
10 gr. linen seeds
10 gr. sunflower seeds
10 gr. pumpkin seeds
10 gr. sesame seeds
100 gr. wheat sourdough starter
11.5 gr. salt
2.5 gr. yeast
1 tbsp. sugar
320 gr. warm water

Directions:

1. Toast all seeds in preheated frying pan without oil until golden. Let them completely cool at room temperature.

2. Add all ingredients to mixing bowl and knead dough with stand mixer until it become smooth and elastic 3 to 5 minutes on the low speed and then 5 minutes more on high speed. Don't overheat the dough. Its temperature should be around 23 °C / 73,4 °F at the end of kneading process.

3. Knead dough into a ball, put into bowl, cover with plastic wrap and keep in fridge about 12 to 16 hours. Dust linen cloth with some flour. After that take dough out of the fridge, divide into pieces and form bread. Transfer it to prepared linen and set aside for 40 minutes covered with kitchen towel.

4. Preheat oven to 230 °C / 446 °F. Slightly spray bread with water and garnish with seed mixture, make cuts and put on baking tray lined with baking paper.

5. Reduce the heat in oven to 220°C / 428 °F and bake bread for 20 to 30 minutes depends of your oven type. Serve it with veggie patties, hummus, stir-fried vegetables and herbs.

FOCACCIA WITH OLIVES AND SUN-DRIED TOMATOES

Focaccia is a one of traditional types of Italian bread. Usually it cooked with black olives which associate with Italian olive trees as symbol of prosperity and richness.

To vary this recipe a little bit we decide to use other favorite Italian ingredients – fresh and sun-dried tomatoes and aromatic basil. If you want to add some piquant notes, use tiny bit of dried chili flakes or spices: oregano, cumin or thyme.

You can easily eat focaccia with different condiments. The best choice in my opinion is to serve it with garlic olive oil, tomato salsa and pesto. Also, you can add some fresh vegetables or avocado and even hummus.

This time we will make sourdough focaccia, but you could make it without sourdough starter with using yeast. The recipe of this delicious full of Italian flavors bread with yeast you will also find in this book.

Ingredients:

400 gr. wheat flour
65 gr. wheat sourdough starter
100 gr. village bread flour
2 tbsp. semolina
300 ml. warm water
2.5 gr. fresh yeast
Pinch of sugar
100 gr. black olives
75 gr. green olives
Pinch of ground rosemary
1 tbsp. sesame seeds
Sun dried tomatoes
Small cherry tomatoes
Fresh basil

Pickled green chili pepper
Sea salt and ground black pepper

Directions:

1. Add all ingredients into mixing bowl and knead dough with stand mixer until it become smooth and elastic for 10 minutes starting from low speed to high. The temperature of dough at the end should be not more than 23 °C / 73,4 °F. Cover it with plastic wrap and put in warm and dry place for 1 hour.

2. Knead dough with your hands for couple minutes, shape into ball and put in fridge for 12 to 16 hours. After dough rested in fridge, take it out and transfer to working surface dusted with some flour. Cut dough in two parts and roll them into balls, cover with kitchen towel and set aside for 40 minutes.

3. Meanwhile slice olives and cherry tomatoes in halves and sundried tomatoes into pieces. Put dough into baking pans lined with baking paper and greased with olive oil. Gently push dough with your fingers to make a flat disk.

4. Preheat oven to 230 °C / 446 °F. Decorate focaccia with olives, cherry tomatoes, sun dried tomatoes, slightly push them into dough, season with some salt, pepper and bake into oven at 220 °C /428 °F until golden. Decorate it with fresh basil, rosemary, pickled peppers and serve.

HOW TO MAKE DOUGH WITH YEAST

For making bread in this book we will not going to use eggs, dairy products and butter.

For preparing simple dough with yeast you can use different types of flour like wheat, rye, oat, corn, buckwheat, bran and etc. It is quite important to observe the proportions as they were given especially because one type of flour can have more gluten than other.

In this section we will learn how to make dough with yeast and how to use it to bake fluffy bread. This type of dough can be used for doughnuts, buns, pies and other delicious things.

Yeast which we use for kneading the dough are leaven sugars contained in flour dividing them in carbon dioxide and alcohol. Carbon dioxide is creating bubbles in dough and as result it doubles in size and get fluffy airy texture. That's why at the end we have such delicious soft and spongy bread.

For dough usually you will need about 20 to 50 grams of fresh yeasts or half of this amount if you use dry yeast for each kilo of flour. Before even starting make bread, check your yeast properly. If they rose nice and quickly, that means you can use them for dough.

Dissolve the yeast in warm water or dairy free milk. The most favorable temperature for them is around 25 – 30 °C / 77 – 86 °F. Cold liquid stops the vital activity of yeasts and prevent dough from rising. However, if water or milk is too hot that can kill the yeast and dough will never rise.

Before making bread, I suggest you sift flour in advance. It will help to remove any lumps and enrich it with some oxygen.

After you knead dough until it become smooth and elastic, cover it with clean kitchen towel and set aside in warm place until it doubles in size. When dough is well rise, knead it a little bit to add air to our bread, then cover again and set aside for same time.

You can use different type of fat for making bread start from vegetable oil to margarine or butter. In our case we will use only dairy free plant-based products – oil and margarine.

There are two ways to make yeast dough. Small kids love fluffy tender buns, so I recommend you choose second one.

For first way you mix all ingredients for dough in one batch. Then it will need to rise and double in size. After that knead dough once more, cover with plastic wrap and let it rise for another hour.

Second method requires a lot of shortening (various fat products like eggs if you use them, butter, sour cream and etc.). You can easily replace them with similar vegan analogs. At first, we need to make sponge (pre-dough).

Pour water or milk in big mixing bowl, add yeast, a little bit of sugar and half of prepared flour (take as much flour as you need for recipe). Mix until combine. Put sponge in warm place for 45 to 60 minutes. During this time yeast mixture will double in size.

Next sponge will start to slowly go down and you should add shortening, salt and knead until dough become smooth and elastic. Cover it with plastic wrap and proof in warm place for about 2 hours. Periodically check dough and if it doubles in size, knead it and make buns or bread.

It is also necessary to keep the relation of ingredients. You should pay special attention to that. Generally, we need flour, shortening and liquid. If you use less flour reduce the amount of liquid and yeast.

All required ingredients should be thoroughly measured and scaled before cooking. Usually for 1 kg of flour you will need about 40 grams of fresh yeast or 20 grams of active dry yeast, 2 glasses of warm milk or water, 2 to 4 tablespoons of vegetable oil, 1 tablespoon sugar and 1 tablespoon of salt. If you use eggs, you could add 2 to 3 of them (maybe less) depends of your preferences and what you want to make. From this amount of dough, you can cook various pastries and bread and enjoy it with your family.

As special option we prepared for you a list of different recipes with yeast.

HEALTHY RYE & BRAN BREAD WITH ROSEMARY AND OLIVES

Bran bread is absolute favorite in ration of people who put special emphasis on healthy eating.

It contents cellulose, vitamins and minerals. It is also good to know that bran bread is very useful for weigh loss (thanks to cellulose) since when you eat it, your organism starts to clean from harmful stuff.

As final stroke I add some spices and olives to elevate the flavor and texture. Let's bake!

Ingredients:

700 gr. dark rye flour
200 gr. wheat bread flour
100 gr. bran flour
2 tsp. sea salt
1 tbsp. sugar
Rosemary leaves
10 green olives
10 black olives
2 to 3 tbsp. sesame seeds
20 gr. fresh yeast or 10 gr. active dry yeast
600 ml warm water
50 ml extra virgin olive oil
2 tbsp. almond milk
1 tbsp. maple syrup

Directions:

1. Prepare sponge (pre-ferment or pre-dough): dissolve yeast in warm water, add sugar, 1 tablespoon wheat flour and keep in warm place for 7 to 10 minutes.

2. Chop olives and rosemary into pieces. In large bowl sift flour with salt, add olives, rosemary and mix well. Pour yeast mixture into pan, add warm water and olive oil and give a good stir. Gradually pour in flour and knead dough until it become smooth and elastic.

3. Roll it into ball, grease with oil, and cover with plastic wrap and put in warm place for 1 hour. During this time knead dough when it rises.

4. Mix almond milk with maple syrup until combine. Line baking tray with parchment paper. Shape round bread and put on baking tray, grease with syrup mixture and sprinkle with sesame seeds. Put paper stencil on top and dust bread with flour. Carefully remove stencil and leave bread for 30 minutes to rise.

5. Make cuts on top of bread and set aside for another 10 to 15 minutes. Preheat oven to 220 ˚C / 428 ˚F. If your oven doesn't have steam function, before baking spray it with water.

6. Bake bread for 10 minutes then reduce heat to 190 ˚C / 374 ˚F and bake it for 20 to 30 minutes more. Just remember that baking time depends of your oven and your preferences.

TIPS:

You can easily make paper stencil with leaves pattern. First of all, draw leaves on baking paper. Then use sharp knife or blade (be careful) to cut leaves and done. Put stencil on top of bread after you greased it with syrup mixture and sprinkled with some sesame seeds and dust with flour. Carefully remove stencil from bread and make cuts on bread and each leave.

ONION BREAD

Despite that some people think that bread is high calorie product (partly it is truth), its benefits highly big for our organism. This bread is containing huge amount of vitamins (E, K, A, В и PP), healthy fats, proteins and minerals: phosphorus, magnesium, potassium, calcium and iodine.

And for today I have very good recipe of delicious aromatic bread with fried onion and potato stock. You can make is also with sourdough by using pre – ferment method and without potato ingredients.

Ingredients:

450 to 500 gr. flour
150 gr. potato stock
2 tbsp. extra virgin olive oil
200 gr. potato puree
1 tbsp. malt syrup or organic honey
10 gr. yeast
1 ½ tsp. salt
1 large onion

Directions:

1. Boil potatoes, drain the stock and slightly cool before using. Take 200 grams of boiled potatoes and mash into puree.

2. In warm potato stock add malt syrup or organic honey. If you don't have any of them on hand, use sugar instead. Add yeast, 1 tablespoon of flour, mix well and set aside for 15 to 25 minutes.

Slice onion into cubes and stir – fry it in preheat pan with olive oil, season with a bit of salt and cook until it become golden. Set aside until it completely cools.

3. Sift flour with salt. In mixing bowl combine potato stock, potato puree, olive oil and mix well until combine. Add flour into several batches and knead dough on the low speed for 5 minutes. Then add fried onion, increase speed and knead for 10 minutes more until dough become smooth and elastic.

4. Grease large bowl with olive oil, put the dough, cover with plastic wrap and set aside in warm place for 1 to 2 hours. Knead dough on table dusted with some flour, divide it into pieces and make bread. Transfer to linen cloth sprinkled with flour and set aside for another 15 to 20 minutes.

5. Line baking pans with baking paper and dust them with some flour. Put bread into prepared baking pans, cover with kitchen towel and set aside for 30 to 35 minutes more. Preheat oven to 230 °C / 446 °F. Make cuts with sharp blade at 45 ° angle.

6. Spray oven with water and bake bread for 5 minutes, then reduce heat to 200 – 210 °C / 392 – 410 ° F and keep baking for 20 to 40 minutes until nice golden color. Check the readiness with toothpick: if it comes out clean and dry, your bread is ready. Completely cool bread before serving.

TIPS:

For greasing I always use the mixture of 1 tablespoon of maple syrup and 2 tablespoons of almond milk. It will help bread to create such nice crispy golden crust.

Before you start to make bread check the quality of your yeast. If your sponge rising well and you see foam on top that means your yeast is good for bread. However, if water will be too hot yeast is going to be killed.

RYE BREAD ROLLS

These cute and delicious bread rolls are perfect for various sandwiches. You can serve them with different sauces, jams, cheeses, fresh vegetables, greens or as addition for soups, salads and other meals.

For making bread rolls you can use various types of flour and spices.

Ingredients:

350 gr. rye flour
150 gr. whole-wheat flour
1 tsp. sea salt
1 tsp. sugar
Rosemary
10 green olives
2 to 3 tbsp. sesame seeds
8 to 10 gr. active dry yeast
300 ml warm water
25 ml olive oil

Directions:

1. Prepare sponge (pre-ferment or pre-dough): dissolve yeast in warm water, add sugar, 1 tablespoon wheat flour and keep in warm place for 7 to 10 minutes.

2. Chop olives and rosemary into pieces.
In large bowl sift flour with salt, add olives, rosemary and mix well. Pour yeast mixture into pan, add warm water and olive oil and give a good stir. Gradually pour in flour and knead dough until it become smooth and elastic.

3. Roll it into ball, grease with oil, and cover with plastic wrap and put in warm place for 1 hour. During this time knead dough when it rises.

4. Mix almond milk with maple syrup until combine. Line baking tray with parchment paper.

5. Divide dough into pieces, form small bread rolls. Make cuts on top of buns and set aside for another 10 to 15 minutes.

6. Preheat oven to 220 °C /428 °F. If your oven doesn't have steam function, before baking spray it with water. Bake bread for 10 minutes then reduce heat to 190 °C / 374 °F and bake it for 15 to 20 minutes more. Just remember that baking time depends of your oven and your preferences.

TIPS:

If you knead dough and it seems that it is not enough flour, don't worry. Sprinkle table with a little bit of flour and keep kneading dough until it reaches required consistency.

SIMPLE SANDWICH BREAD

Usually sandwich bread contains big amount of sugar, but this recipe requires not so much just for taste.

I like to play with ingredients combination and sometimes replacing water with coconut, soy or any other plant based milk for velvety smooth flavor. When you use dairy free milk, bread becomes whiter and sweeter to taste, with amazingly soft and spongy texture.

This type of bread is perfect for making sweet or savory sandwiches especially when you planned to have a picnic or want to have fast and easy snack.

Ingredients:

850 gr. all-purpose wheat flour
500 ml. warm water (or plant based milk, also warm)
20 gr. dry yeast
80 ml. olive oil
½ tsp. sea salt
80 to 100 gr. white cane sugar

Directions:

1. In warm water add sugar and yeast, give a good stir and set aside for 15 minutes in warm place until yeast well rise.

2. Sift flour into big mixing bowl, add salt. Whisk a little bit until just combine, make a hole in the middle and pour in sugar and yeast mixture. Add olive oil and mix well.

3. Knead dough by your hands until it become smooth and elastic.

4. Shape it into a ball. Cover with plastic wrap and set aside in warm place for 1 to 1,5 hours. Dough should double in size.

5. Line baking pans with parchment paper and dust it with flour.

6. Divide dough into pieces and shape into bread. Put in baking pans, cover with kitchen towel and leave for 40 to 45 minutes to rest.

7. Preheat oven to 220 °C / 428 °F, spray it with water.

8. Bake bread into oven at 180 °C / 356 °F for 35 to 45 minutes until nice golden color. Baking time depends of your oven type, so it is better to check bread periodically.

BASBOUSA

Basbousa is traditional pie in Jewish cuisine. It is symbolizing the prosperity of family, contentment and happiness.

This dessert has tender and moist texture with rich nutty flavor. It is perfect for various celebrations, friend parties or as fast snack with tea.

One of the best parts of this pie is sweet syrup. When you pour it on top, Basbousa absorbs all the flavors and as result it have such delicate moist texture and sweet taste.

Ingredients:

1 ½ cup of wheat flour
1 ½ cup of semolina
½ cup (85 gr.) of brown cane sugar
½ cup (117 gr.) of white cane sugar
100 gr. soy yogurt
½ cup almond milk
½ cup of orange juice
Zest of one orange
50 gr. coconut dairy – free butter
10 to 15 walnuts
1 tbsp. baking powder
1 tsp. baking soda
1 tbsp. vanilla extract
1 tbsp. rose water
1 tsp. cinnamon
½ tsp. sea salt
Pinch of nutmeg
Pinch of ground anise star

For syrup:

1 cup of white cane sugar
½ cup of organic honey or syrup

Juice and zest of 1 lemon
50 gr. coconut dairy – free butter

Directions:

1. Whisk coconut dairy – free butter with sugar for 5 to 7 minutes, add soy yogurt and almond milk, zest and juice of orange, vanilla extract, rose water, cinnamon, anise, nutmeg and mix until combine. Peel walnuts. Try to not break them.

2. Sift flour with baking soda and baking powder, add semolina and mix well. Combine dry ingredients with liquid mixture. Give a good stir. Make sure that there are no lumps in batter.

3. Preheat oven to 190 °C / 374 °F. Grease baking pan with coconut butter, dust with some flour and discard any excess. Also, you can line bottom with baking powder. Pour batter into baking pan, knock pan on the table to remove air bubbles. Put walnuts on top and slightly push them into batter.

4. Bake pie for 40 minutes or until wooden stick comes out clean and dry.

5. Meanwhile make the syrup.

6. Mix sugar, lemon juice and coconut butter in saucepan. Place on the medium – high heat and cook until sugar is dissolved. Remove from the heat, slightly cool, add honey, syrup and zest of lemon. Mix well and pour on top of pie.

FOCACCIA BREAD WITH SUNDRIED TOMATOES AND OLIVES

Focaccia can be with or without yeast. Without yeast it will be crispier and crunchy.

Aromatic focaccia bread with spices, olives and sundried tomatoes, with airy tender texture and amazing flavors. So delicious that you simply couldn't resist to not to treat yourself with a bit of this amazingly tasty delicacy.

Of course, it is better to give bread some time to infuse the flavor, but you can serve it warm with cup of freshly brewed coffee or tea.

Focaccia is one of the oldest types of bread. In antiquity it was made for villagers and warriors. In age of ancient Roman Empire, they used to make flatbreads in remaining ash from bonfire, very similar to modern focaccia.

It is recommended to add garlic and fresh herbs in end of baking process or they will burn out.

Focaccia can be sweet or savory, with various condiments and spices. For example, in north Italy serve it sweet with fruits, syrups and other sweet toppings. In south Tyrol traditionally cook focaccia with potatoes and rosemary.

But I decide to make my own version.

Before serving, I suggest you drizzle focaccia with olive oil.

Ingredients:

400 gr. all – purpose flour
100 gr. village flour
2 tbsp. fine semolina
300 ml warm water
15 gr. active dry yeast
1 tsp. of sugar
150 to 200 gr. black olives
2 tbsp. olive oil

Some sprigs of rosemary
1 tbsp. sesame seeds
Small cherry tomatoes
5 – 6 sun dried tomatoes
4 large garlic cloves
Sea salt and ground black pepper

Directions:

1. In jug or glass mix together yeast with sugar and 70 ml of water, give a good stir and put in microwave (do not turn it on). Place a cup of hot boiling water next to yeast mixture, close door and let it sit for several minutes.

2. Mix olive oil with remaining warm water. Sift flour into a bowl, add semolina, sesame seeds, sugar, salt and whisk until combine. Make a hole in the middle and pour in yeast mixture and oil with water. Thoroughly mix and then knead dough until it become smooth and elastic.

3. Shape it in ball, put in bowl, cover with plastic wrap and keep in warm place 40 to 50 minutes until it doubles in size.

4. Roughly chop peeled garlic, sun dried tomatoes and olives. Cut cherry tomatoes in two halves.

5. Preheat oven to 200 °C / 392 °F. Put dough in baking pan greased with olive oil. Align it with your fingers. Middle part should be slightly thinner than sides because it will rise when you bake.

6. Decorate focaccia bread with olives, sun dried tomatoes, garlic and cherry tomatoes slightly push them with your fingers. Sprinkle with rosemary, season with some salt and pepper, cover with kitchen towel and place in warm place for 30 minutes.

7. Bake bread in preheated oven 30 to 35 minutes or until toothpick comes out clean and dry.

8. Take out bread from the oven, transfer to wire rack and let it cool for 5 to 10 minutes.

9. Serve with garlic oil.

TIPS:

If you want to make focaccia softer, add plant – based milk in dough instead of water.

CINNABONS

There are so many varieties of this culinary masterpiece of 20th century. Cinnabons were invented by father and son Rees and Greg Colin from Seattle, Washington, USA.

Cinnabons are absolutely perfect as meal for breakfast. Delicious cinnamon rolls with tender but chewy texture combined with sweet milky glaze (dairy – free, of course) and amazing spicy aroma that makes you feels a bit calmly and cozy. As pleasant addition you can drizzle them with chocolate or cream glaze and serve them with warm hot cocoa or milk tea and just relax and enjoy your time.

Ingredients:

Dough:

450 gr. all-purpose wheat flour
250 ml **warm soy or coconut milk**
2 tsp. active dry yeast
3 tbsp. warm water
3 tbsp. sugar
1 tsp. vanilla essence
¼ tsp. salt
1 tbsp. corn or canola oil
50 ml soy yogurt
50 ml melted coconut butter

Greasing:

2 to 3 tbsp. almond milk
1 tbsp. maple syrup

Filling:

100 to 150 gr. brown cane sugar
3 tsp. ground cinnamon

Glaze:

1 cup icing sugar
¼ tsp. vanilla essence
3 tbsp. almond milk
1 tbsp. vegan cream cheese

Directions:

1. Combine one half of warm milk with melted coconut butter, add vanilla essence, water mix well and set aside in warm place. Make pre – ferment (pre-dough) with yeast (follow same method which was written before), sugar and remaining warm milk. Leave it for 15 minutes in warm place. Then combine prepared pre-dough with liquid ingredients.

2. Sift flour into mixture, add a bit of salt and knead until dough become smooth and elastic. If you have stand mixer it will be way easier to use it for this step.

3. Cover dough with kitchen towel and put in warm place for 1 hour. After that time knead it once more for couple minutes with your hands, cover with kitchen towel and set aside in warm place for another 30 to 40 minutes. Dust working surface (your table or countertop) with flour and roll dough in flat rectangle, about 5 – 7 mm. (0.2 inch) thickness.

4. Combine sugar with cinnamon and sprinkle it all on top of dough. Carefully wrap dough in roll. Cut into pieces about 3 cm. (1.1 inch) thickness. Line baking pan or tray with parchment paper. Put cinnabons into lined baking pan. Mix almond milk with maple syrup and use it for greasing buns. Let them sit in warm place for 30 minutes. They should double in size.

5. Meanwhile preheat oven to 180 ˚C / 356 ˚F. Bake buns in oven for about 15 to 20 minutes, depends of your oven type. While cinnabons are baking, make the glaze. Combine all ingredients in a bowl and mix until combine. Completely cool cinnabons before glazing. Serve them with a cup of tea, hot chocolate, coffee latte or other your favorite drinks. Enjoy!

BREAKFAST SESAME BUNS

This recipe is super easy to make but requires some patience and time. To cook these buns, you will need about 3 hours for rising and baking but during that time you can do anything what you need.

You can cook these lovely buns in different ways: with or without adding plant – based milk, with raisins, nuts, various spices, seeds or chocolate. Crunchy and crispy outside but spongy and tender inside – these cute breakfast buns perfectly go with any kinds of drinks and toppings.

Ingredients:

Dough:

1 cup coconut milk
2 ½ cups all-purpose wheat flour
½ cup warm water
2 tbsp. coconut oil
2 tbsp. olive oil
2 tbsp. sugar
½ tsp. salt
2 tsp. active dry yeast

Greasing:

2 tbsp. coconut milk
1 tbsp. agave or maple syrup
2 tbsp. sesame seeds

Directions:

1. In warm water add 1 tablespoon of sugar and yeast, stir and set aside in warm place for several minutes. In a saucepan combine coconut milk with sugar, salt, coconut and olive oil. Place it over medium heat and wait until coconut oil is completely melts. Remove from the heat.

2. Sift flour into large bowl, make a hole in the middle and pour in yeast and milk mixture. Mix well and then knead dough until it become smooth and elastic. You can use stand mixer for this process. Cover dough with plastic wrap and put in warm place for 1 hour until it doubles in size.

3. Knead dough one more time, cover with plastic wrap and set aside in warm place for another hour.

4. Dust table or working surface with flour. Knead dough once more on dusted table. Divide it in 7 – 8 balls and roll them into buns.

5. Line baking tray with parchment paper. Mix coconut milk with syrup until combine. Put buns to baking tray with some space between them, cover them with kitchen towel and set aside for 30 minutes until they double in size.

6. Preheat oven to 190 °C / 374 °F. Grease buns with prepared syrup mixture, sprinkle with some seeds on top and bake into oven for 15 to 20 minutes depending of your oven type.

7. You can serve these lovely buns with cup of freshly brewed tea or coffee and strawberry jam.

STRAWBERRY JAM

Delicious homemade sweet jam made from fresh juicy strawberries and amazing blend of spices. You can use it in various desserts, as toppings or even mix it with cream.

I love to use it as sauce for banana pancakes or serve it with freshly baked breakfast buns.

Ingredients:

300 gr. strawberries
200 gr. white cane sugar
2 small cloves
5 gr. pectin powder
1 cardamom seed
¼ tsp. cinnamon
Juice of one lemon

Directions:

1. Mix sugar with pectin.

2. Slice strawberries into cubes, put into saucepan, add sugar and pectin mixture and set aside for 1 hour.

3. Place it on medium – high heat, drizzle with lemon juice, add spices and mix well. Bring mixture to boil and let it simmer until jam start to thicken.

4. Remove from the heat and completely cool before serving. Enjoy!

TRADITIONAL JEWISH BREAD
CHALLAH

Challah is delicious white braided loaf which traditionally use as decoration by Jewish people for Sabbath. Usually this recipe includes eggs but today we will make it suitable for vegans or people who can't eat eggs due to some reasons.

You can also use this kind of dough for buns or bread, but I think that it will be more delicious if you make a traditional braided challah.

Ingredients:

800 gr. wheat flour
25 gr. sugar
180 gr. soy yogurt
60 gr. extra virgin olive oil
1 ½ tsp. salt
250 gr warm water

For greasing:

2 tbsp. almond milk
2 to 3 tbsp. maple syrup

For sprinkling:

Sesame seeds
Poppy seeds

Directions:

1. In a jug combine sugar, yeast, 160 grams of flour, add 250 ml warm water and give a good stir until combine. Cover with plastic wrap and set aside in warm place for 20 minutes. Mix soy yogurt with olive oil and put in warm place.

2. Sift flour with salt in large bowl, add prepared yeast mixture, yogurt with olive oil and mix well until combine. Knead dough to make it smooth and elastic about 10 to 15 minutes (if you want, use stand mixer).

3. Roll dough into a ball, grease with some olive oil and put in large bowl, cover with plastic wrap and set aside in warm place for 1 hour. Knead dough once more, cover again and set aside for another 40 minutes.

4. After dough double in size, transfer it to table or working surface dusted with some flour, knead it and divide in 2 or 4 parts depends of the size of bread which you want to make. Divide each part in 3 pieces, roll them into balls and cover with kitchen towel.

5. Line baking tray with baking paper. Roll each ball into long sausage and plait into braid. Carefully transfer challah to prepared baking tray and set aside for 30 to 40 minutes to rise. Preheat oven to 180 °C (356 °F). Mix all ingredients for greasing in small bowl.

6. Grease challah with prepared mixture, sprinkle with sesame seeds and poppy seeds. Bake for 30 to 40 minutes. When challah will be ready, take it out from the oven, cover with kitchen towel and completely cool on the wire rack. After it completely cool serve challah to table.

ORANGE GINGER CAKE

My book is dedicated to bread, but I also want to share the recipe of this wonderful cake with you.

Orange and Ginger Cake is ideal when you want to change something in your menu and cook delicious but simple treat which will be perfect for kids and adults. Wonderful taste and nice moist texture of this dessert make it good as pair to aromatic herbal tea, jam sauce or chocolate syrup.

Ingredients:

250 gr. all – purpose wheat flour
100 gr. brown cane sugar
350 gr. liquid honey (you could replace it with syrup)
140 gr. applesauce
40 ml vegetable oil
20 ml melted coconut dairy – free butter
80 ml orange juice
Zest of lemon and orange
½ tsp. cinnamon
½ tsp. ground pink pepper
½ tsp. ground ginger
½ tsp. baking powder
1 tsp. baking soda
1 tsp. fine sea salt
2 pinch ground cloves
Pinch of ground nutmeg
Few grams of grated fresh ginger

Directions:

1. Mix orange and lemon zest with orange juice and grated ginger in a bowl.

2. Sift flour with soda and baking powder into mixing bowl, add spices, brown sugar and salt, and mix well.

3. Add honey (or syrup), orange juice mixture, oil, coconut butter and whisk until combine.

4. Line sides and bottom of baking pan with parchment paper, slightly grease it with coconut butter and dust with some flour (remove all excess).

5. Pour batter into prepared baking pan. Preheat oven to 200 °C (392 °F). Bake cake into oven for 45 to 50 minutes.

6. Take it out and completely cool on wire rack. Sprinkle cake with icing sugar, decorate with some flowers and serve.

TIPS:

For this cake we use 20 cm. (7.8 inch) baking pan, but if you choose 15 or 16 cm. baking pan, cake will be taller, and you will need to regulate the cooking time according to size of your baking pan.

HOMEMADE BURGER BUNS

As all of you know that for making burgers first of all you need buns. You can buy them in supermarket but, trust me, it will be so much better if you make them by yourself.

Burgers are one of the popular snacks in world. There are so many varieties how you could cook or serve them. However, good burger requires best quality bun. It is quite important to choose it right with thick but soft texture and nice taste. This recipe of Homemade Burger Buns is easy to follow and don't take much time. Just remember that if dough is too liquid add some flour or if it is too thick pour in a bit of olive oil.

Nevertheless, I highly recommend you to not overdo with flour. If dough contains too much flour it become dry and hard when it's bakes. Also, if you want to color your buns, add liquid color gel in first batch with liquid ingredients or you can skip that.

Ingredients:

350 gr. bread wheat flour
230 gr. warm plant based milk
7 gr. of yeast
1 tbsp. cane sugar
50 gr. extra virgin olive oil
Black food color "Americolor"

For greasing:

2 to 3 tbsp. almond milk
1 ½ tbsp. maple syrup
Sesame seeds

Directions:

1. In warm milk add yeast and sugar. Mix well and put in warm place until they rise. Meanwhile yeast are rise sift flour in mixing bowl. Add salt and mix everything with whisk until combine.

2. In yeast mixture add olive oil, give a good stir and pour in dry ingredients. If you want to make black buns add black color gel into liquid and then pour in flour.

3. Knead dough for some time then transfer it to table dusted with some flour and keep kneading until it become smooth and elastic. Also for this process you could use stand mixer. Combine all ingredients in mixing bowl, turn mixer on and mix on the low speed for 2 minutes. Then turn it off, scrape dough from the sides of bowl and knead with mixer gradually increasing speed. When dough start to looks like ball turn it off.

4. Put it in bowl greased with some olive oil, cover with plastic wrap and keep in warm place for 1 hour until it doubles in size. Then knead it once more, cover again and set aside for another 30 minutes.

5. Put dough on scales and weigh it. Then transfer it to table dusted with some flour and divide into same size pieces. Roll them into balls, cover with kitchen cloth and let them rise about 30 minutes.

6. Line baking tray with parchment paper and dust it with some flour. Mix almond milk with maple syrup and set aside. Put buns on lined baking tray, grease with almond milk mixture, sprinkle with sesame seeds and set aside for another 30 minutes. Preheat oven to 180 °C / 356 °F. Bake buns into oven for 15 to 20 minutes depends of your oven type. Take them out from the oven and cool on wire rack.

CINNAMON BUNS

What will perfectly go with afternoon tea or cup of freshly brewed coffee? Delicious aromatic Cinnamon Buns with tender texture and sweet taste. Super soft dough "clouds" with spicy cinnamon fragrance reminds me time when I was a little girl and help my mom to cook and bake.

Dough for this recipe is quite easy to make but requires some time to rise. To speed up this process use the method with microwave which we used before for yeast.

These cinnamon buns you can serve with butter and apricot jam (don't forget to dust them with a bit of icing sugar) or if you want to cook them in healthier way use a steamer.

Ingredients:

1 cup coconut milk
2 ½ cups all – purpose flour
½ cup warm water
2 tbsp. coconut oil
2 tbsp. olive oil
2 tbsp. sugar
½ tsp. salt
2 tsp. active dry yeast
1 tsp. cinnamon

For greasing:

1 tbsp. maple syrup
2 tbsp. almond milk

Directions:

1. In warm water add one tablespoon of sugar and yeast, stir and set aside in warm place for 5 to 7 minutes for rising.

2. Pour coconut milk in saucepan, add remaining sugar, salt, coconut and olive oil. Place on the medium heat and cook until coconut oil completely melts. Remove from the heat.

3. Sift flour in large bowl, add cinnamon, pour in yeast mixture and warmed milk. Mix well and then start to knead dough until it become smooth and elastic. It is quite important to thoroughly knead dough until you reach ideal consistency and it starts to easily stick out from your hands. Put dough into a bowl, cover with plastic wrap and keep in warm place for 1 hour until it doubles in size. Knead it once more, cover again and put in warm place for another hour.

4. Dust table with some flour and knead dough on top of it for 5 minutes, divide it into 7 to 8 balls and make buns.

5. Line baking tray with parchment paper. Put buns on baking tray with some space between them and cover with clean kitchen cloth.
Prepare greasing mixture by mixing all required ingredients. Grease buns with milk and syrup liquid.

6. Preheat oven to 190° C / 374 ° F. Bake buns into oven for 15 to 20 minutes and completely cool before serving.

VEGAN STEAMED BUNS WITH APPLE AND PEAR FILLING

This recipe of delicious Vegan Steamed Buns with Apple and Pear filling is one of the healthy and nutritious options for breakfast, lunch or dinner.

These cute buns are very simple to make by following the recipe which we wrote and as result you will gain sweet and soft buns with airy texture and juicy caramel fruit taste. You can serve them with any type of drink and at any time in a day.

We use the natural bamboo steamer, but you can use the regular steamer. Just make sure that you have special paper liners for it.

Ingredients:

For dough:

1 pack of active dry yeast (11 gr.)
1 ½ cup almond milk
2 tbsp. coconut oil
2 tbsp. white organic sugar
1 tsp. cooking sea salt
4 cups all – purpose wheat flour

For filling:

2 sweet pears
2 to 3 green apples
Cinnamon
Nutmeg
3 to 4 tbsp. organic white sugar
50 to 70 gr. raisins
2 tbsp. honey liqueur Jack Daniels
Juice half of lemon
1 tbsp. coconut oil

Directions:

1. For filling wash and dry the raisins, soak in honey liqueur Jack Daniels.

2. Cut apples and pears into cubes. Add sugar to non – stick frying or saucepan. When it's become light brown, add apples and pears. Stir well.

3. Sprinkle with 1 tablespoon of sugar, drizzle with lemon juice and mix well. Cook for several minutes and add raisins. Season it with some spices, coconut oil and stir with spatula. Remove from the heat and allow it completely cool.

4. For dough warm up the almond milk until it reaches approximately 26 – 28 °C / 78,8 – 82,4 °F . Add sugar, yeast, and set aside for 5 minutes.

5. Sift flour into a large mixing bowl, add raised yeast mixture, coconut oil and salt. Mix well with spatula until dough start to stick together.

6. Knead the dough, cover with clean cloth and put in warm place for 1 hour.

7. When the dough is double in sizes, knead it once more, cover with cloth and keep in warm place another 40 minutes.

8. Divide dough into 12 balls. Stuff buns with prepared fillings, close the edges, cover with wet cloth and set aside in warm place for 30 minutes.

9. Line bamboo steamer with paper liners, put buns, grease them with almond milk and steam for 15 minutes. Make sure that you tightly close the last section of bamboo steamer with wet cloth.

10. Grease prepared buns with apricot jam, sprinkle with sesame seeds, poppy seeds, cinnamon and serve.

FLUFFY BUNS WITH CARAMELIZED APPLES & CRUMBLE

A few words about baking

Each of us basking in the warmth of the day under the warm blanket and watching good films dreamed of something delicious.

Or gathering a cheerful friendly company we are often puzzled by what we cook and how to treat the guests with something delicious.

And in this difficult situation baking always helped us, from year to year. Varied buns, gingerbread, cakes, cakes, muffins, cookies. All this adds to our lives a bit of happiness.

I often remember my childhood. The smell of cinnamon and vanilla, the aroma of fresh buns with raisins and freshly baked golden bread, twisted into braid, sprinkled with poppy seeds, sesame seeds or fried onion. As it seems to me, it is impossible to forget these scents and sensations. Even now, when I write about this, I have before my eyes these rainbow-colored pictures and involuntarily getting hungry.

How to determine the quality of flour?

First of all, good quality flour must be dry and odorless. Determine the moisture content of flour in a simple way: just squeeze it in your hand. If after you have released your hand the flour has retained its original form of handful it is too moist. Dry flour should immediately disintegrate. The dryer the flour the more delicious and better your pastry or baking.

Before consumption flour should always be sifted. When sifting the flour, it is saturated with oxygen, and the dough is obtained by air, and the finished products acquire a softer taste.

How to add sugar?

Sugar should be added in a moderate amount because too much sugar in the test leads to the fact that the baking burns and badly baked. Therefore, it is important to follow exactly the recipe prescription and follow the dosage.

If you are vegetarians and consume dairy products, you could add to dough butter and eggs. As I wrote before, not everyone in my family follows vegan lifestyle, but I often cook something tasty for my children. And it's doesn't matter what kind of race, eye or skin color we have. The only two things are important: love and tolerance.

However, sometimes to realize that and accept the weakness and merits of other people, the years should pass. And if your friend, brother, sister or neighbor is vegan or meat eater, make two types of dough and share these delicious buns with your family and friends.

Ingredients:

For dough:

430 to 450 gr. all-purpose wheat flour
200 ml. warm plant-based milk
8 gr. dry yeast
75 gr. sugar
1 tsp. chia seeds
45 gr. dairy free butter
1 tbsp. extra virgin olive oil
1 tsp. vanilla extract or vanilla paste
½ tsp. sea salt

For caramelized apple filling:

3 to 4 apples
30 gr. dairy free butter
1 tsp. dark rum
2 cinnamon sticks
1 anise star
100 gr. raisins

2 tbsps. lemon juice
35 to 40 gr. cane sugar
Ground cinnamon

For biscuit crumble:

50 gr. wheat flour
30 gr. dairy free butter
30 gr. white cane sugar

For glaze:

2 tbsps. soy milk
2 tbsps. maple syrup

Directions:

1. Sift flour in mixing bowl. In plastic or glass jug add sugar, yeast, some flour and warm plant-based milk. Set aside for 5 to 10 minutes. Melt butter and cool at room temperature.

2. In mixing bowl with flour make a hole and when yeast mixture is raised well, add to flour. Pour in melted dairy free butter, add chia seeds and salt and knead dough until it become smooth and elastic for 10 to 15 minutes. Do not add excess flour.

3. Grease clean mixing bowl with olive oil, put dough, cover with plastic wrap and place in warm place for 1 hour 30 minutes.

4. Divide dough in pieces, about 70 to 75 grams each, cover with kitchen towel and set aside for 30 to 35 minutes.

5. Peel and slice apples in cubes, remove seeds and drizzle with lemon juice. Wash raisins and dry with paper towel.

6. In frying pan add dairy free butter, apples, raisins, anise and cinnamon sticks. Cook about 5 to 7 minutes, add sugar, some cinnamon and mix well. Remove from the heat.

7. Combine ingredients for biscuit crumble until it's start to looks like bread crumbs.

8. Mix everything for glaze until combine.

9. Preheat oven to 180 °C / 356 °F.

10. Make a hole on top of buns with glass, sprinkle with cinnamon, put some apple filling and set aside for 30 minutes.

11. Grease with glazing mixture, sprinkle with biscuit crumble and bake in preheated oven for 15 – 20 minutes (depends of your oven type) or until nice golden color. Completely cool before serving.

12. Serve with plant-based milk, hot chocolate or herbal tea.

BIRD BREAD

I want to share with one easy recipe of cute fluffy golden bird-shaped buns. Traditionally these cuties made on Easter holidays. From this dough you can also make nice bread muffins, pies, soft bread and stuffed buns.

Ingredients:

500 ml warm water
900 gr – 1 kg wheat flour
11 gr. dry yeast
¾ glass of sugar
1 tsp. vanilla sugar
1 tsp. salt
½ glass of olive oil
Raisins (for eyes)

For greasing:

Sweet black tea

Directions:

1. Let's make yeasty dough.

2. Mix sugar with yeast and warm water. Set aside for 5 to 10 minutes. Meanwhile sift flour into mixing bowl, add salt, vanilla sugar and whisk well.

3. Make a hole in the middle and pour in yeast mixture, add oil and knead dough until it become smooth and elastic.

4. Cover bowl with plastic wrap and let dough rise in warm place for 1 hour. Then knead it a little bit, cover again and set aside in warm place for another 40 minutes.

5. Roll dough into long sausage and divide it into 40 same weight parts. Roll each piece into long stripe, about 15 cm. length. Tie stripe into a knot and shape one end like bird head. Slightly flatten the other end and cut it to make it look like bird tail. Make eyes from raisins (slice each one into small pieces).

6. Line baking tray with baking paper. Transfer birds to baking tray, cover with clean kitchen towel and set aside in warm place for 20 to 30 minutes.

7. Preheat oven to 180 °C / 356 °F. Grease birds with sweet tea and bake 20 to 25 minutes. Put them on the wire rack and completely cool after baking.

8. Serve.

BAGELS

Bagels are one of traditional Jewish food which was brought to United States by Jewish and now it is definitely belongs to vegan cuisine.

We will cook them in two ways. One of them was my mothers and aunt recipe and another one is what I use every time when I want to make bagels. You can try them both and choose that one which you will like the most.

Ingredients:

First way:

For dough:

500 gr. wheat flour
7 gr. active dry yeast
5 tbsp. white cane sugar
2 tsp. salt
150 ml warm water
100 ml warm coconut milk
2 tbsp. extra virgin olive oil

For sprinkling:

Sesame seeds
Poppy seeds
Gold linen seeds

For grease:

2 tbsp. almond milk
1 tbsp. maple syrup

Directions:

1. Slightly warm up water, add coconut milk, one half of sugar and yeast, mix well, cover with plastic wrap and keep in warm place for 15 minutes.

2. Sift flour into mixing bowl, add salt, yeast mixture and mix well until combine. Transfer dough on table dusted with some flour and knead it until it become smooth and elastic.

3. Grease mixing bowl with oil. Roll dough into ball, slightly grease it with olive oil and put into prepared mixing bowl. Cover it with plastic wrap and keep in warm dry place for 1 hour until dough doubles in size.

4. Dust table with flour, take out dough from mixing bowl and put it on table, knead it until it become nice and smooth. Weight dough on scales and divide in 12 to 15 pieces, roll them into balls. In each ball make a hole with your finger and slightly spin it around. Cover bagels with kitchen towel and set aside for 35 to 40 minutes until they double in size.

5. Preheat oven to 190 °C / 374 °F. Grease baking tray with oil and dust with flour. Mix almond milk with syrup until combine.

6. In large pan add water, sugar and bring to the boil. Carefully transfer bagels to pan and cook on medium heat for 10 minutes. Don't put too much.

7. Take out bagels from pan using skimmer to remove excess water and put them on baking tray, grease with syrup mixture, sprinkle with seeds (or fried onion) and bake into oven for 30 minutes. Remove baking tray from oven, cover with kitchen towel and set aside for several minutes. Then serve bagels with different toppings, vegetables or fruits.

Ingredients:

Second way:

For dough:

500 gr. wheat flour
7 gr. active dry yeast
5 tbsp. white cane sugar

2 tsp. salt
150 ml warm water
100 ml warm coconut milk
2 tbsp. extra virgin olive oil

For sprinkling:

Sesame seeds
Poppy seeds
Gold linen seeds

For grease:

2 tbsp. almond milk
1 tbsp. maple syrup

Directions:

1. Prepare yeast mixture according to previous recipe instructions. Combine all remaining ingredients in mixing bowl. Add yeast mixture, turn stand mixer on and knead dough for 15 minutes periodically scrape it from sides of bowl.

2. When dough start to looks like ball, gradually add in olive oil. If dough is too thick, add 1 tablespoon of water and knead it for 2 to 3 minutes.

3. Roll dough into ball, put into mixing bowl, cover with plastic wrap and keep in warm place for 30 minutes. Then knead it for 5 minutes, cover again and put into fridge.

4. Dust table with flour and put dough on it. Knead it for 2 to 3 minutes, divide into pieces and roll them into balls. Make hole in the middle of each ball and put them on baking tray lined with baking paper.

5. Cover balls with kitchen towel and set aside in warm place until they double in size.

6. Preheat oven to 220 ˚C / 428 ˚F, then reduce heat to 180 ˚C / 356 ˚F. Mix almond milk with syrup until combine.

7. In large pan add water, sugar and bring to the boil. Carefully transfer bagels to pan and cook on medium heat for 10 minutes. Don't put too much.

8. Take out bagels from pan using skimmer to remove excess water and put them on baking tray, grease with syrup mixture, sprinkle with seeds (or fried onion) and bake into oven for 30 minutes. Remove baking tray from oven, cover with kitchen towel and set aside for several minutes.

9. You can serve bagels with vegan cream cheese, guacamole, avocado, peanut butter and jam, fresh fruits and vegetables. Try different combinations and choose your favorite. Bon Appetite!

CINNAMON TWISTED BREAD

Fascinating cinnamon aroma, crunchy golden crust and tender and spongy center – this yummy cinnamon twisted bread is better to serve with glass of cold dairy – free milk or cup or fragrant herbal tea.

Cinnamon twisted bread, also known as Estonian Kringle, is a very popular European dessert. Even though it seems hard to make, you can easily cope with that by using our recipe.

Ingredients:

650 gr. all – purpose wheat flour
3 tbsp. white cane sugar
10 to 11 gr. active dry yeast
30 gr. extra virgin olive oil
1 tsp. sea salt
300 ml warm water

For filling:

½ tsp. brown cane sugar
2 to 3 tsp. cinnamon

For greasing:

3 tbsp. syrup
2 tbsp. almond milk

Directions:

1. In measuring jug add sugar, yeast, 160 grams of flour and mix well. Add 250 ml warm water, give a good stir and set aside in warm place for 15 to 20 minutes.

2. Sift flour with sea salt into large mixing bowl, pour in prepared yeast mixture (sponge), add remaining warm water, mix well and start kneading dough until it become smooth and elastic.

3. Make ball, grease it with oil, pun into bowl and cover with plastic wrap or kitchen towel. Keep dough in warm place for 1 hour. When it doubles in size, knead it, cover with towel and set aside for another 40 minutes.

4. Line baking tray with parchment paper.

5. Roll dough into rectangle, dust with sugar and cinnamon mixture and make roll. Cut it lengthwise but don't reach the end on one side. Twist dough into braid, connect two ends with each other and carefully transfer to baking tray. Set aside for 30 to 40 minutes.

6. Preheat oven to 180 ˚C / 356 ˚F. Mix almond milk with syrup until combine.

7. Grease twisted cinnamon bread with almond milk mixture and bake into oven for 30 to 35 minutes.

LIVE WITHOUT GLUTEN

In our world there are a lot of different people with various lifestyles: meat eaters, vegetarians, pescatarians, vegans, raw eaters and etc. Nevertheless, many of these trends were invented because of certain illnesses and allergies on some kinds of food.

For example, term 'vegetarianism' appeared in the beginning of 20 century. Vegetarian diet was designed to patients who have allergy on animal and dairy products. Thereafter, vegetarianism became very popular lifestyle of many people around the world.

So, what is 'gluten free diet'?

To answer on this question, we need to know what gluten is. Gluten is a mixture of proteins. Principally, it contains in wheat, rye and barley. Gluten hasn't any analogs in plants. Thanks to its compound dough become smooth and elastic during the kneading process.

Unfortunately, some people should avoid gluten products, especially when they have celiac disease or allergy on gluten.

Despite that, gluten free diet has its own benefits:

Reducing of consumption refined products: fats, pastry, fried food and unhealthy desserts.

Increasing of energy.

Normalization of cholesterol level.

Healthy weight loss.

Gaining the nutritious value from fruits, nuts, vegetables and grains.

Cleaning of organism

Decreasing the risk of heart disease and diabetes.

Of course, someone could think that gluten free diet is too ordinary, boring and doesn't have such delicious things like desserts or such simple food like pasta or bread. But there is no need to draw a hasty conclusion, because today you can find various gluten free analogs in your supermarket or make them at home.

WHY GLUTEN IS HARMFUL?

People who have celiac disease or allergy on gluten must remove all products with gluten because this disease of digestive system could be cured only by decreasing any gluten products, especially bread and pastry.

In this book we paid special attention to bread and pastry, that why in this chapter you will find interesting and healthy recipes without gluten.

GLUTEN FREE DARK BREAD

We will start to make gluten free bread from delicious recipe of dark bread with dried fruits.

This type of bread is easy to make and you can add to it various seeds or olives, dried tomatoes and herbs. But for now, we will bake it with chewy dried fruits that will create a wonderful taste and pleasant aroma.

Ingredients:

500 gr. dark gluten free bread flour
425 ml. soy or other plant-based milk
20 gr. chickpea flour + 60 ml. water or 2 egg whites (if you consume eggs)
2 tsp. active dry yeast
1 tbsp. sugar
5 tbsp. olive oil
1 tsp. apple or wine vinegar
½ to 1 tsp. fine sea salt
35 gr. dried apricots
35 gr. dried cherries
30 gr. raisins
5 to 10 gr. gluten free flour for dried fruits
120 ml dark rum or orange juice

Directions:

1. Soak dried fruits in rum or orange juice (about 120 ml.) and set aside for 1 hour.

2. In warm plant-based milk add sugar and yeast, mix well, cover with plastic wrap and put in warm and dry place.

3. Mix chickpea flour with water until combine or whisk egg whites until fluffy. Add apple vinegar, sea salt, 4 tbsp. olive oil, mix well. Pour in raised milk and yeast mixture, give a good stir and set aside.

Drain the liquid from dried fruits, dry them with paper towel and mix with gluten free flour.

4. Add flour to mixing bowl, pour in liquid mixture and knead with hook attachment for 5 minutes on the low speed. Scrape the dough from sides of mixing bowl, add dried fruits and knead for 10 minutes on the medium – high speed. Add remaining oil and knead for another 5 minutes.

5. Grease baking pans with oil and dust with some gluten free flour. Remove the excess flour and line the bottom of pans with baking paper.

6. Divide dough into 3 parts and put in pans. Cover with clean kitchen cloth and let it rise in warm place for 40 to 60 minutes. Preheat oven to 220 °C / 425 °F.

7. When dough is raised enough, bake bread in oven for 50 to 60 minutes, depends of your oven type and its possibilities. Check it with wooden stick or toothpick.

8. Completely cool bread before serving.

GLUTEN FREE GREEN BUCKWHEAT BREAD

Gluten free bread made of green buckwheat flour, have a strong nutty flavor and thick airy texture. This bread is so tender, fluffy and not only delicious but also nutritious and healthy alternative to white bread.

It perfectly goes with spices and aromatic herbs, sundried tomatoes, fried garlic or onion, nuts and seeds and etc. We will make it with some pumpkin seeds and olives, but you can choose any other ingredients according to your preferences.

If you don't have green buckwheat flour, you can make it by yourself with coffee or nut grinder or stand mixer with special attachment "mill" which you can find in Kenwood or Kitchenaid mixers.

Ingredients:

500 gr. green buckwheat flour
400 gr. warm water
8 gr. yeast
25 gr. sugar
½ tsp. salt
50 ml olive or grapeseed oil
100 gr. olives
Handful or pumpkin seeds
5 to 10 gr. gluten free flour for olives

Directions:

1. In mixing bowl add water, yeast and sugar. Mix well, cover with plastic wrap and set aside for 10 to 15 minutes.

2. When yeast is raised enough, add flour, salt, oil and knead dough with hook attachment for 5 minutes on the low speed.

3. Meanwhile, chop olives into pieces, mix with pumpkin seeds and gluten free flour. Add to dough and keep kneading for another 10 to 15 minutes on the medium – high speed. Don't forget to periodically scrape dough from sides of mixing bowl. Dough should be slightly wet, but that is fine.

4. Grease baking pan with oil, dust with some flour and line the bottom with baking paper. Fill baking pans with dough about 1/3 part. Dust with some buckwheat flour on top and cover with kitchen cloth or towel. Let bread rise for 45 minutes to 1 hour.

5. Preheat oven to 220 – 230 °C / 428 – 446 ˚F.

6. Make sure that bread is not become flat. When it is raised enough, immediately place it in preheated oven. Spray oven with some water & reduce the heat to 180 – 190 °C / 356 – 374 ˚F and bake for 25 minutes, depends of its size.

7. Cool on wire rack before serving.

TIPS:

Also, you could divide dough in two parts and make one bread with olives and another one with dried fruits.

GLUTEN FREE ZUCCHINI BREAD

Delicious gluten free bread full of nutritious value, vitamins and minerals. Nice and smooth zucchini flavor make it perfect for savory or even sweet sandwiches. For this recipe you could also use carrot instead.

Ingredients:

1 large grated zucchini
3 tsp. (30 gr.) sugar
63 ml (¼ cup) water
1 ½ tsp. chia seeds
1 ½ tsp. linen seeds
2 tbsp. sunflower seeds
65 gr. buckwheat flour
45 gr. oat flakes
70 gr. oat flour
40 gr. rice flour
30 gr. cornstarch
¼ tsp. salt
Pinch of nutmeg
4 tbsp. almond milk
2 tbsp. baking powder
½ tbsp. apple cider vinegar
2 tbsp. vegetable oil

Directions:

1. Line baking pan with greaseproof paper. Preheat oven to 180 °C / 356 °F.

2. Grate zucchini with grater. Use grater with big holes.

3. n a separate bowl mix water, baking powder, sugar, seeds, vinegar and oil. Mix well until combine, then place in fridge for 15 to 20 minutes.

4. In mixing bowl add flour, sifted cornstarch, oat flakes, salt and nutmeg. Give a good stir with whisk until there are no lumps in mixture.

5. Add one half of grated zucchini into liquid mixture and one half to dry ingredients. Mix well.

6. Combine two mixtures in a bowl. Make sure that batter is thick but not too much. Add almond milk and give a good stir.

7. Pour batter into baking pan, line it with spatula to create nice and smooth top. Bake into oven for 50 to 55 minutes. Check the doneness with toothpick.

8. Cool the bread into pan for 10 minutes, and then carefully transfer it to wire rack and set aside until it completely cools.

9. Serve with stir – fried vegetables and freshly chopped herbs.

STIR - FRIED VEGETABLES WITH FRESH HERBS

These vegetables can be served not only as condiment for bread but also as a perfect addition to any kind of side dishes. Red onion and leek are ideal combination for colorful juicy cherry tomatoes. As nice accompaniment we used bright and sweet bell peppers.

If you like spicy food as we do, add red hot chili pepper. To elevate the taste of the meal, I recommend to use green chili pepper which you clean from the seeds and slice into long stripes. This method will add a bit of piquant flavor to vegetables but won't make them too spicy.

Ingredients:

1 red bell pepper
1 yellow bell pepper
1 orange bell pepper
1 red onion
1 leek
1 lime
3 garlic cloves
12 to 15 multicolored cherry tomatoes
½ bunch of fresh coriander and parsley
1 green chili pepper (optional)
Mint leaves
Olive oil
Sea salt, freshly ground black pepper

Directions:

1. Thoroughly wash all vegetables and dry before usage. Remove the core and seeds from bell peppers, slice them into cubes or triangles.

2. Clean green chili pepper and cut into stripes. Finely chop fresh coriander and parsley.

3. Cut cherry tomatoes into halves, season with some salt, black pepper, drizzle with lime juice and little bit of olive oil. Sprinkle with chopped herbs and set aside. Slice leek into circles and red onion into petals.

4. Add olive oil into preheated nonstick frying pan, add pressed garlic and cook until it become golden. Remove with skimmer. Transfer sliced red onion to frying pan, stir – fry until it become transparent, season with some salt, drizzle with lime juice and mix well.

5. After 2 minutes add bell peppers, mix well and cook until half done. Add green chili pepper and leek, mix well. Put one half of cherry tomatoes and cook for 2 minutes. Remove from the heat, add remaining tomatoes, drizzle with lime juice, olive oil and sprinkle with some chopped herbs.

6. Slice the bread, put nice spoon of stir-fried vegetables on top and serve.

GLUTEN FREE SANDWICH BREAD

This bread is perfect for anything. You could use it for making sandwiches, toasts, croutons, breadcrumbs and anything you want to do.

My favorite combination is nice but thin layer of dairy – free butter and good dollop of thick strawberry jam. Gorgeous combination with cup of green tea.

Ingredients:

Liquid ingredients:

2 tsp. sugar
1 cup (200 ml) warm water
¾ cup (60 ml) almond milk
3 tbsp. vegetable oil
2 ½ tbsp. linen seeds
2 tbsp. chia seeds
2 tsp. dry yeast
2 tsp. apple cider vinegar

Dry ingredients:

1 cup (130 gr.) corn flour
1 cup (133 gr.) buckwheat flour
½ tsp. sea salt
1 tsp. baking powder
½ tsp. baking soda

For garnish:

2 tsp. sesame seeds
2 to 3 tbsp. pumpkin seeds

Directions:

1. Preheat oven to 180 °C / 350 °F. Line baking pan with baking paper.

2. In separate bowl mix yeast with sugar, seeds and warm water until combine. Set aside for 5 minutes. Add almond milk and oil, give a good stir and set aside.

3. Combine flour, salt, baking soda and baking powder in mixing bowl, mix well with whisk and add liquid mixture. Mix on the medium speed with spatula attachment until batter become smooth.

4. Put batter into lined baking pan, sprinkle with seeds on top and bake for 50 to 55 minutes.

5. Transfer to wire rack and let it completely cool. Serve with strawberry or berry confiture.

STRAWBERRY CONFITURE

You could cook strawberry confiture in different ways: with or without spices, citrus zest or only with sugar.

This recipe is good if you want to store strawberry confiture more than 2 to 3 months. It will be perfect as a filling for donuts, pies and cookies or as a great addition for cream.

Ingredients:

1 kg strawberries
1 kg sugar
¼ tsp. ground cardamom
¼ tsp. ground cinnamon
Pinch of nutmeg
Juice of one lemon

Directions:

1. Put strawberries into saucepan, add sugar, drizzle with juice of ½ of lemon and set aside overnight. It is necessary to squeeze a juice from berries.

2. Place saucepan with strawberries on the medium – high heat and bring mixture to the boil, carefully remove all foam and cook for 5 minutes. Set aside covered with lid overnight.

3. Place saucepan on the medium – high heat, add remaining lemon juice, cardamom, cinnamon and nutmeg, mix well and bring to the boil. Cook for 5 minutes, remove from the heat and pour into different jars. Tightly close them with lids.

4. Cover table with clean kitchen towel. Turn jars upside down and set aside until strawberry confiture is completely cool. Make sure that you close lids very tightly because if you not do it properly, berry syrup will leak out.

5. Keep jars in cold and dry place.

6. Serve this confiture with scones, buns, donuts or cookies.

CHOCOLATE GLUTEN FREE MUFFINS WITH FROSTING

Delicious sweet dessert with twist of walnuts and small touch of coffee - Chocolate Gluten Free Muffins with frosting. Rich taste of chocolate, nice moist tender texture and amazing chocolate cream make it perfect as a treat for parties or family holiday dinner.

Also, you can serve them with various drinks, but I prefer a glass of refreshing & chilling Iced Matcha Almond Latte.

Ingredients:

For muffins batter:

200 gr Medjool dates
240 gr water
35 gr cocoa powder
1 tbsp. ground coffee
1 tsp. vanilla extract
1/2 tsp. ground cinnamon
1 tbsp. baking powder
Pinch of salt
130 gr. oat flour (or ground oat flakes)
80 to 100 gr. almond milk

For frosting:

200 gr. Medjool dates
2/3 cup of almond milk
1 tbsp. peanut butter
125 gr. melted dark chocolate
1 tbsp. maple syrup
1 tbsp. cocoa powder
1 tbsp. cacao butter

For decorating:

Almond flakes
Sugar sprinkles

Directions:

Chocolate Muffins:

1. Add Medjool dates and water into blender, mix until smooth. Add all remaining ingredients and mix on low speed until just combine.

2. Fill cupcake tins until 3/4 of their volume. We used thick cardboard cupcake cups because paper cups are not good for these purposes. Carefully knock it on the table to remove any air bubbles.

3. Preheat oven to 180 °C / 350 °F.

4. Bake these cute little guys for 25 to 27 minutes. If you have a gas oven, I highly recommend to put a baking pan with water on the bottom of your oven. It will prevent cupcakes from burning.

5. Completely cool them before decoration.

Chocolate Frosting:

1. Melt chocolate on bain - marie, add syrup, cacao butter and peanut butter, mix well until combine.

2. Add dates and almond milk to the blender and mix until smooth.

3. Add remaining ingredients and whisk once more until you reach nice creamy consistency.

4. Decorate cupcakes with chocolate frosting, sprinkle with some sugar sprinkles and almond flakes.

GLUTEN FREE SCONES WITH POPPY SEEDS

When nice weather is outside, it is perfect time to have a walk, take a breath of amazing aroma of blooming flowers and enjoy pleasant atmosphere of spring. Also, you could make wonderful picnic with delicious sandwiches, warm tea from thermos and something sweet for dessert like scones.

Scones are one of most popular kind of British pastry. Traditionally, they served with jam and clotted cream or butter. But today we will make gluten free version.

Ingredients:

1 cup oat flour
1 cup (130 gr.) buckwheat flour
½ cup (60 gr.) coconut flour
¼ cup (54 gr.) cane sugar
½ tsp. fine sea salt
1 tsp. baking powder
2 tbsp. poppy seeds
1/3 cup (90 gr.) cold coconut oil
¾ cup (125 ml) almond milk
Zest of one lemon
¼ tsp. cinnamon

For glaze:

1 cup (250 gr.) icing sugar
5 – 6 tbsp. almond milk

For serving:

Strawberry jam
Orange jam
Candied lemon zest

Directions:

1. Preheat oven to 200 °C / 392 °F. Line baking tray with greaseproof paper.

2. In large bowl mix flour, sugar, baking powder, salt, cinnamon, poppy seeds and lemon zest. Transfer mixture to food processor.

3. Add solid coconut oil and grind until mixture start to looks like breadcrumbs.

4. Add almond milk and mix until combine. If dough is too liquid, add a bit of buckwheat flour. Knead dough for 5 minutes, make a disk and cover it with plastic wrap. Put in fridge for 15 minutes.

5. Roll dough in 4 cm. thickness (about 1.6 inch). Cut scones with round cookie cutter and transfer them to prepared baking tray. Bake into oven for 15 to 20 minutes or until toothpick comes out clean and dry.

6. Remember that baking time depends of your oven type and its possibilities.

7. Transfer scones on wire rack and let them completely cool before glazing. Mix sugar with almond milk until combine. Pour glaze on top of scones, sprinkle with some poppy seeds, add a bit of jam and candied lemon zest on top and serve with green mint tea. Enjoy!

OAT BREAKFAST MUFFINS WITH DRIED APRICOTS

Let's make delicious and wonderful muffins without gluten for breakfast. To elevate the flavor and texture, we will add some dried apricots soaked in dark rum.

This recipe is pretty simple but at the end we get tasty breakfast or snack dish without spending too much time or ingredients. Just couple minutes, a little bit of passion and healthy meal is ready.

Ingredients:

2 pinches saffron
2 tbsp. chia seeds
2 tbsp. oat flakes
230 gr. chopped dried apricots
2 to 3 tbsp. dark rum (optional)
60 gr. oat flour
100 gr. corn flour
120 gr. walnuts
100 gr. orange juice
Pinch of salt
190 gr. applesauce or apple puree
2 tbsp. cane sugar
1 tbsp. melted coconut oil
1 tbsp. corn oil
2 tbsp. almond milk
1 ½ tsp. baking powder
1 tsp. vanilla extract
Almond flakes for decorating

Directions:

1. Put saffron in orange juice, mix well and set aside for 5 to 10 minutes. Add chia seeds, give a good stir and put in fridge for 1 hour or if you want to leave it overnight.

2. Toast nuts into oven without oil for 5 minutes at 180 °C / 356 °F. Slightly cool them and roughly chop into pieces.

3. Put dried apricots in a bowl, add rum and vanilla extract, mix and set aside.

4. Combine all ingredients in food processor, add dried apricot mixture and stir well. Put batter into thick cupcake paper cups or greased muffin tins. Don't forget to dust tins with a bit of flour before you will put the batter. That will help to easily remove muffins from tins and prevent them from burning.

5. Sprinkle with some almond flakes on top.

6. Preheat oven to 180 °C / 356 °F. Bake muffins for 20 to 25 minutes. Check with toothpick.

7. Completely cool before serving. Serve these oat muffins with cup of coffee, tea or your favorite drink. Enjoy!

TIPS:

If you want to make muffins fluffy, add 2 teaspoons of baking powder. Also, ¼ teaspoons of turmeric give them nice sunny color.

LEMON DRIZZLE CAKE

The secret of perfect lemon cake is pretty simple but in the same a bit of fancy. There are some important details, which are necessary to achieve and ideal result: rich but balanced flavor, moist and delicate texture, nice smooth shape.

Lemon cake shouldn't be crumbly, too sweet or too sour. Every ingredient must harmonize and complement each other to create a beautiful symphony of taste, aroma and shape.

Nevertheless, this recipe is absolutely multipurpose, because you could replace lemon with berries, oranges, apples, dried fruits, chocolate and any other things.

Ingredients:

Liquid ingredients:
100 gr. (1/2 cup) coconut oil
125 gr. (1/2 cup) + 2 tbsp. sugar
180 ml (3/4 cup) warm almond milk
60 ml (1/4 cup) lemon juice
Zest of two lemons
Zest of one orange
1 tsp. vanilla extract

Dry ingredients:
170 gr. (1 ½ cup) gluten free cake clour
¾ tsp. baking soda
1 tsp. baking powder
56 gr. almond flour
44 gr. rice flour
2 tbsp. poppy seeds
¼ tsp. cinnamon

For glaze:
½ cup icing sugar
5 – 6 tbsp. lemon sugar

For decorating:
Candied lemon zest
1 tsp. poppy seeds
2 tbsp. fresh cranberries

Directions:

1. Preheat oven to 180 °C / 356 °F.

2. Mix coconut oil with sugar with hand mixer until smooth. Add almond milk, lemon juice, vanilla extract, zest or orange and lemon.

3. Sift gluten free flour, baking powder and baking soda into mixing bowl. Add poppy seeds, cinnamon, rice and almond flour. Mix with whisk until combine.

4. Add liquid mixture and give a good stir. Batter should be smooth and without lumps.

5. Line round baking pan with baking paper and grease the sides with vegetable oil, sprinkle with some flour and remove any excess flour. Pour batter into baking pan, use spatula to make it smooth on top and then knock it on top of the table to remove air bubbles.

6. Bake into oven for 50 minutes. Check with toothpick.

7. Transfer cake on the wire rack and let it cool for another 20 minutes. Mix icing sugar with lemon juice until combine. Pour the glaze on top of cake and set aside for 5 minutes.

8. Decorate with poppy seeds, cranberries and candied lemon zest. Serve with freshly brewed black tea or iced latte.
Enjoy!

METRIC CONVERSION CHARTS

Liquids:
55 ml - 2 fl oz
75 ml - 3 fl oz
150 ml - 5 fl oz
257 ml - 10 fl oz
570 ml - 1 pint
725 ml - 1 1/4 pint
1 liter - 1 3/4 pint

Measuring spoons in ML:
1/2 tsp. - 2.5 ml
1 tsp. - 5 ml
1/2 tbsp. - 7.5 ml
1 tbsp. - 15 ml

Cups in ML:
1/4 cups - 60 ml

1/3 cup - 80 ml

1/2 cup - 120 ml

1 cup - 240 ml

A **pinch** is equal to **1/4 tps.**

A **handful** is equal to **1/4 cup**

Liquid ingredients to 1 cup equivalent (gr):

1 cup water, milk, juice, etc. - 225 ml

1 cup oils - 215 ml
Grams in Ounces:
250 gr - 9 oz
500 gr - 1 lb 2 oz
1 kg - 2 1/4 lb
2 kg - 4 1/2 lb

Made in United States
Troutdale, OR
01/10/2024

16862263R10131